Photographs:

Barbara Hucková
Miroslav Hucek

Text:

Václav Cibula
Petr Chotěbor
Alexandr Kliment
Eduard Škoda

dNit DEElc

PRAGUE

ILLUSTRATED
GUIDE

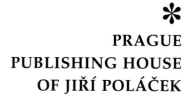

**PRAGUE
PUBLISHING HOUSE
OF JIŘÍ POLÁČEK**

CONTENTS

I. PRAGUE

In history the chief town of the Czech principality and kingdom and since 1993 the metropolis of the Czech Republic, Prague, is a unique architectural whole created through out long centuries. We can thank a happy combination of circumstances, the great foresight of its founders and the immense sensitiveness of a whole number of architects and builders for the multiform and ever surprising appearance of the city.

The basic conditions lay in the unusually favourable modelling of the terrain, which made the founding of a naturally protected ruler's seat possible and afforded sufficient space for settlement on both banks of the Vltava. In the initial period it was not the question merely of a relatively small area for building-up, but mainly of a kind of reserve for the future growth of the town. The intersection of long-distance routes at the ford across the Vltava was definitely a very important element. The suitability of the place for the founding of a town is indirectly confirmed by archeological findings pertaining to older settlement on the territory of Prague and the idea of building a castle site in its nearest environs.

The founding of Prague Castle as the fortified seat of the Czech princes in the last third of the 9th century was decisive for the origin of the town. Settlement of comparable age is archeologically documented in the western outer bailey of the Castle and on the territory of the present Little Quarter (Malá Strana) to the south of it. True, the other fortified castle of the princes, Vyšehrad, was not originally a seat as the legend about the Princess Libuše tells us, but it was used already in the 10th century. Vyšehrad formed the natural southern boundary of the continuous settlement on the right bank. However, apart from concentrated inhabitation in the environs of Prague's market-place, a number of small separate communities, often with churches, some of which have remained, existed on the territory of present Prague.

The Romanesque period saw the development of Prague, particularly during the reign of Vladislav II. Large and dominant buildings (for example, Strahov Monastery) increased in number and a stone bridge, called Judith's Bridge, demonstrated the maturity of the town. A number of stone houses sprang up on the territory of the older Old Town, some of them having the form of separately standing courts, while others respected the street front.

The Gothic style penetrated into Prague only slowly from the second third of the 13th century. One of the first Early Gothic buildings was the convent of the Poor Clares and Minorites „Na Františku", built from 1233. During the reign of Václav I the Old Town was fortified and it was only later that so-called Gall's Town (Havelské město) also became a part of it. The Little Quarter underwent a great change – Přemysl Otakar II had the original population moved away and replaced it with German colonists in 1257. The fortifications of the Little Quarter were connected up with the territory of Prague Castle.

In 1291 the Old Town was destroyed by a great fire, its renewal being realized on the new level of the terrain (the Old-New [Staronová] Synagogue in Židovská Street, for example, marks the older one). In 1296 the Old Town applied for the right to found a Town Hall, but its request was not granted.

The Luxembourg period practically completed the building-up of the historic core of Prague. In the early 14th century the built-up area of the western outer bailey was transformed into the newly founded tributary town of Hradčany with fortifications. The Old Town had to be renewed after another fire in 1316, high Gothic buildings now prevailing. Apart from a number of important sacral and dwelling ones (the best-known of them is the house At me Bell – U zvonu), the reign of John of Luxembourg brought

about another important change in the Old Town: in 1338 the king permitted the purchase of a house in Old Town Square (Staroměstské náměstí) and founding of Town Hall. A number of progressive measures was adopted (paving of the streets, the replacement of wooden arcades with masonry ones) and a trade centre also originated (cloth stalls, butchers' shops).

The further development of Prague was fundamentally influenced by Charles IV by the founding a university in 1348 and (in the same year) the

Praga caput regni – Prague the head of the kingdom – says the proud inscript on this Renaissance window of the **Old Town Hall.** The window of the present Wedding Hall originated after 1526 and its side parts date in the thirties of the 18th century. In the hemispherical tympanum above there is the emblem of the Old Town of Prague in a heraldic arrangement.

The Rotunda of St. Mary at Přední Kopanina is a Romanesque building of the first half of the 12th century. It has a typical hemispherical apse and a high steeple in westerly direction. In 1818 its vault collapsed and in the fifties of the 19th century its interior war repaired and newly vaulted. In the 19th century its interior was repaired and newly vaulted. On the high altar there is a relief The Crucifixion of the 16th century and a painting by Josef Helich from 1861.

laying of the foundation stone of the New Town. His fortifications demarcated a huge territory making future development possible. The New Town (Nové Město) represents a well-thought-out summit medieval project with its main axes and a large market-place (Senovážné Square, the Horse Market – Wenceslas Square (Václavské náměstí) and the Cattle Market – Charles Square (Karlovo náměstí). The network of churches of older communities was supplemented with newly founded sacral buildings. The largest building was to be the Church of Our Lady of the Snows, of which only the presbytery was completed. The changes made at Charles IV's time also involved the left bank. Further territory was attached to the Little Quarter by the construction of a new sector of the fortifications – the so-called Hunger Wall. After the destruction of Judith's Bridge during the flood of 1342 Charles IV had a new stone bridge built under the supervision of Peter Parler. The bridge tower in the Old Town is outstanding not only for its architecture, but also for its exceptional sculptured decoration.

At the time of Václav IV a number of his father's buildings was completed. The king built a new, permanent seat in the Old Town – the King's Court. Apart from this, he had Hrádek „Na Zderaze" built on the territory of the New Town.

The following restless period of the Hussite wars was not suitable for building activity. On the contrary, it meant a number of losses for the towns of Prague. The Little Quarter and Vyšehrad were practically destroyed and Prague Castle sustained damage. Even after the mid-15th century Prague had few more important buildings (the Little Quarter bridge tower, the tower of the New Town Hall, the Powder Tower). The earliest Renaissance, which appeared in the Jagiello reconstruction of the Castle, left only negligible traces in the town.

Renaissance architecture manifested itself in mature buildings constructed by numerous Italian artists who had settled in Prague as late as the mid-16th century. Space was mainly created for them by a destructive fire which occurred in the Little Quarter, at the Castle and in Hradčany in 1541. Not only new houses, but also large and imposing palaces of the aristocracy were erected, for example, Lobkovitz (now Schwarzenberg) and Martinic Palaces in Hradčanské Square, or the palace of the lords of Hradec on the New Castle Steps. Numerous Renaissance reconstructions also enriched houses in the Old and the New Town. The decision of the Emperor Rudolph II to make Prague his permanent place of residence (from 1583) had a positive influence on the development of Prague. After his death the imperial court moved to Vienna and after the short episode of the uprising of the Estates, Prague witnessed the merciless punishment of the defeated. A number of aristocratic and burghers' families, often wealthy and cultured, emigrated. As usual, the long period of the Thirty Years War was unfavourable for the development of the towns, but the wealthiest of the post-war newly-rich nevertheless built in Prague. Due to its size the new Valdštejn Palace, built from 1623 on the site of a larger number of Little Quarter houses, represented a wholly unique complex. Three years later the construction of the Loretto place of pilgrimage was started at Hradčany. According to an imperial decree of 1653 Prague became one of me main fortresses in Bohemia and gained new fortifications with bastions, built at great cost for a long time still. Building activity fully developed after the Thirty Years War. New palaces of the nobility, monasteries

View from a spire of St. Vitus's Cathedral. In the foreground the southern wing of Prague Castle, in the centre of the photograph Malostranské Square with St. Nicholas's Church and behind it the greenery of Kampa, Marksmen's and Slavonic Islands. Behind the Vltava the New Town and on the horizon the tower buildings on the Pankrác plain. Visible among the greenery is Legion Bridge. On the right upstream of the river, is Jiráskův Bridge and behind it the railway bridge. ▶

The interior decoration of the **Old-New Synagogue** is supplemented with a tall standard fixed to a pillar of the main nave. The Jewish community was granted the right to carry its own pennon by Charles IV. The Jewish standard gained its present form through its restoration in the time of Charles VI. on the occasion of the birth of his son, Archduke Leopold, in 1716. In the centre of the pennon there is the six-sided star of David with a Jewish hat, the emblem of Prague Jews for centuries.

and churches sprang up in Early Baroque style after designs by Italian architects. Often huge, outwardly austere buildings originated (for example, the Clementinum or Černín Palace). After 1700 the approach of Baroque artists underwent a substantial change. Instead of massive Early Baroque ones they erected buildings in the dynamic Baroque style which were designed for a given place and with a view to their environs. The design of an ostentatious whole, but also perfect details and a considerable amount of sculptured façade decoration were typical. Baroque architecture culminated with the work of K. I. Dienzenhofer, who designed and realized a whole number of remarkable buildings in Prague of which mention should at least be made of St. Nicholas's Church in the Old Town and the completion of the church consecrated to the same saint in the Little Quarter. In general it can be said that the Baroque gained complete mastery over Prague and radically changed its appearance as a whole. Many older dominants of the Middle Ages remained, however, the image of the town being lent well-thought-out finishing touches and supplements. The feeling for the Baroque prevailed in Prague practically to the end of the 18th century.

The new style, Classicism, penetrated slowly into Prague, manifesting itself only in a few unique buildings (the Estates Theatre, the U Hybernů Customs house, the Church of the Holy Rood in the street Na Příkopě). Prague also experienced other changes. Joseph II's reform resulted in Prague's four towns being connected into one whole. In the early 19th century the area of the town, demarcated by fortifications, ceased to suffice and natural growth and planned founding of suburbs (Karlín in 1817, Smíchov in 1838) came about. Considerable attention was devoted to transport (the second, chain bridge across the Vltava, Chotkova Road, bringing of the railway into the town, Karlín viaduct), and also to public greenery (Chotkovy Park, opening of the Royal Enclosure to the public). Romantism asserted itself already from the first half of the 19th century in connection with an admiration for history and inspiration from historic models in new building activity.

After the mid-19th century great popularity was enjoyed by pseudo-historic styles, it being the Neo-Renaissance that in Prague experienced the greatest flourish (the National Theatre) and later its specific stream, the so-called Czech Baroque, based on domestic architectural monuments of the 16th century. After the Prussian-Austrian war the fortress statute was abolished and demolition of the fortifications began, this making linking-up with the suburbs and suburban communities, which had originated (Bubeneč, Holešovice, Libeň and others) possible.

Typical 19th-century buildings included apartment houses and, as regards public buildings, mainly schools, stations and pension institutes. Apart from the important monuments which were repaired in this period (in the spirit of historism and architectural purism), historic buildings were demolished and replaced with new ones in several places. It was the New

On 14 July, 1420 the Hussite captain Jan Žižka of Trocnov defeated the Crusaders of King Sigismund of Luxembourg on this site. Thanks to the ingenious fortifications on the hill and the enthusiasm of the defenders the first expedition of the Crusaders against Bohemia failed. In the years 1927 to 1932 the **National Monument** was built on the summit of Vítkov. A sculptured landmark of Prague, a bronze equestrian statue of the victorious military commander, stands in front of it. The monument, sculptured by B. Kafka, is 9 metres high and weighs 16.5 tons.

Until 1948 Prague was the centre of large industrial exhibitions – the Prague Sample Fairs. In 1924 the **Trade Fair Palace,** an outstanding work of Czech constructivism, was built after a project by O. Tyl and J. Fuchs for exhibition purposes. The palace has eight floors above ground and two below ground level. A large exhibition hall with galleries and an imposing court passes through all the floors, in 1974 the Trade Fair Palace was greatly damaged by fire, being adapted in later years for the collections of modern art of the National Gallery.

Town that underwent the greatest change, but the realization of considerable measures in other parts of the town was also considered. In 1893 the clearance law was approved on whose basis practically the whole of the Josefov quarter (the former Jewish Town) and the Vojtěšská quarter were changed.

Although pseudo-historic forms continued to survive it was the Art Nouveau that ruled building activity shortly after 1900, leaving in Prague both monumental public buildings (the Municipal House, Wilson Station) and a number of apartment houses. Less in number but important are Prague's cubistic buildings, mostly built before World War I. This style was followed by so-called rondocubism (an arched style), which was to become a kind of „national style" of the new republic. From 1. 1. 1922 11 formerly separate towns and 26 separate communities were attached to the historic core, giving rise to so-called Great Prague. This whole was divided into 19 quarters and administered by a magistrate's office subordinated to the mayor. Prague's State Regulation Committee influenced the development of the new whole mainly from the urban aspect. A. Engel's project for Vítězné Square in Dejvice can be mentioned as an example of an important modification in the period between the two world wars.

During World War II the historic core of Prague (apart from the destruction of the Old Town Hall) fortunately remained a historical reserve. This fact later excluded drastic changes and established a firm order for building activity on a strictly defined area. Historic architectural buildings were subjected to systematic research, which was the essential precondition for their correct restoration. However, apart from successful and sensitively realized reconstructions, measures were taken which were unsuitable for a monument. The idea of rapid and cheap housing construction led to

Prague being surrounded by a ring of housing estates with prefabricated blocks of flats. The advantage – possibly the only one – lies in all of them lying an adequate distance from the historic core of the city. Even so, however, the silhouette of Prague was also spoiled by a number of tower buildings (for example, edifices in Pankrác) which are too massive (the Palace of Culture), or too technical (the Žižkov transmitter). Fortunately, the unsuccessful modern buildings in the historic core are more or less unique (the National Assembly, the New Stage of the National Theatre). In general the nationalization of apartment houses was reflected in their inadequate maintenance.

After the fundamental changes of November 1989, manifested not only in changes of the names of streets, numerous of houses have returned to private hands. A rapid process of development of building activity began which is liquidating the results of neglected maintenance and modernization. However, this activity is also a threat to the architectural purity of Prague. True, the city should not be a museum or a skanzen, but even as a vital metropolis it must preserve its monuments and the unique atmosphere for which it is so appreciated and sought-after. The given problems, which are numerous (at random transport, the living environment, public greenery, the obsolete engineering network, cleanliness, the liquidation of waste) must essentially always be solved with a view to the interests of the city as a whole. The fact that Prague was placed on the UNESCO list of monuments in 1993 was an expression not only of its value, but also of its enormous commitments for the future.

II. THE ROYAL ROUTE

The photographer Miroslav Hucek walked along the Royal Route in Prague a thousand times in order to prepare the most interesting photographs for our „Guide". Thus we can believe him when he says that Prague – that is the Royal Route and all the other places, which are connected with or intersect this historic axis of the city.

So far no one has determined the time at which this attractive name for the route between the Powder Gate (Prašná brána) and St. Vitus's Cathedral at the Castle caught on. The route, which runs across Charles Bridge (Karlův most), was also once called the Coronation Route. A millennium of history came to an understanding with the citizens of the Old Town (Staré Město) in Czech, with the merchants and craftsmen of the Little Quarter (Malá Strana) in German and Italian and with the wealthy rabbis in Hebrew that this route would be called the Royal Route, because the solemn processions of Czech kings passed this way. For the first time the parents of our king and Roman emperor Charles IV – John of Luxembourg and Eliška Přemyslovna – in 1311. For the last time in 1836 on the occasion of the coronation of Ferdinand V. These processions are documented by both word and picture and we even know what financial demands they made on the three towns of Prague. For example, the coronation of John of Luxembourg and Eliška cost the people of Prague 120 talents of silver for the jewels and 600 talents for the realization of the historic event in general.

Everyone in Prague knows the course of the Royal Route, but white letters on red panels indiciate only the names of the squares and streets forming the individual sectors of the route: Celetná Street, Old Town Square (Staroměstské náměstí), Karlova Street, Mostecká Street, Malostranské náměstí, Nerudova Street and the street called Ke Hradu running to the Hradčany ramp, from where the whole of this route can be observed. It naturally also takes us across Charles Bridge, which spans the River Vltava.

A hurrying pedestrian can cover the Royal Route in one hour, but that who wants to enjoy an unforgettable experience, to delve into history a bit, to employ his fantasy and also to relish something good from a glass or a plate spends a whole day following the Royal Route. And he will return to it. An experienced photographer, a diligent enterpreneur or a poet taking a walk alone the Royal Route would confirm that it is beautiful in every hour of the day and night and in every season of the year. And in all weather conditions. With a full or an empty purse or wallet. And in every mood. For those who live here permanently the Royal Route remains something special throughout their whole lifetime. We can always discover something new here.

From the Powder Gate to Charles Bridge the Royal Route runs through Celetná Street, across Old Town Square and along Karlova Street to the right bank of the River Vltava to the Square of the Crusaders with a Red Star (Křižovnické náměstí), which laymen and art historians alike consider to be the most beautiful even if the smallest square in Prague. This is the first third of our Royal Route. We divide it into three parts. The second part is Charles Bridge itself, while the third part is formed by the Little Quarter and the way to the Castle. Celetná Street of the present was originally called Celetná Street after the plaited rolls (calty) and bakers (caletníky) who baked them here already in the 13th century. They had someone to offer them to. A long time previously a trade route had passed this way from East Bohemia to Prague's markets and clerks and officials hurried this way bearing messages to the Castle.

The picturesque façades mostly date in the Baroque and Rococo periods, but the houses behind them conceal Renaissance ceilings and Gothic and Romanesque masonry and vaults, below which we can still sit and imagine how people banqueted here whole centuries ago. For instance, in house No. 11/598, called „At the Golden Stag" (U zlatého jelena) or house No. 2/553, called „At the Sixts" (U Sixtů), where beer was tapped already in the 16th century. In 1547 the owner of the latter house, Sixt of Ottersdorf, took part in the uprising of the Czech Estates against Ferdinand Hapsburg. In 1618 his son Jan Theodor repeated the rebellion against the Hapsburgs and after the Battle of the White Mountain he emigrated for reasons of faith. The house was purchased by the governor's scribe Filip Fabricius, who was also thrown from a window of Prague Castle during the defenestration in 1618. And a moving history is attached to every house.

W. A. Mozart sojourned in Celetná Street and Josefína Dušková, a singer and Mozart's frequent hostess, was born here. In 1848 the renowned philosopher and mathematician Bernard Bolzano died here and it was here, in the same revolutionary year, where the incident which gave rise to the armed uprising of the citizens of Prague took place in front of the military headquarters in Prague. Four hundred barricades originated in Prague overnight, but they were not able to resist the superior forces of General Windischgrätz.

Celetná Street can boast not only with a long-standing tradition, but also with modern originality. Standing on the corner opposite the former mint is the first cubistic house in Europe. It was built in 1912 by the architect J. Gočár. Its architecture blends beautifully with the surrounding historic buildings and the attentive pedestrian will be surprised by the fact that the same brilliant architect erected completely insensitively a functionalistic building for the world-known footwear manufacturer Baťa between the palace of Caretto Millesimo (No. 13, of 1750 on Romanesque and Gothic foundations) and the palace of the Manhart family (No. 17). However, even this contrast is historical and confirms the fact that the Royal Route accepted with all objectivity the role of a witness to the millennium of development of Prague.

At the end of Celetná Street it is necessary to make haste in order to be in time to watch the parade of the Apostles on the astronomical clock on the Old Town Hall. This attractive piece of theatre takes place on the stroke of ever hour. Old Town Square is a big theatre stage where the dramas of Prague and indeed of the whole Czech kingdom have taken place. It was just here where on 14. October, 1918 the people of Prague assembled in order to demand the formation of a republic. The square enthusiastically applauded solemn speeches and witnessed cruel executions. In February 1948 the working-class Prime Minister Klement Gottwald proclaimed the communist regime from the balcony of Kinský Palace and in 1990 President Václav Havel announced from the same balcony that a thick fullstop had been put to the communist epoch. In 1422 the radical Hussite leader Jan Želivský was executed here and after the defeat in the Battle of the White Mountain (1620) twenty-seven Czech lords were executed in the square as representatives of the anti-Hapsburg rebellion. Their names and titles can be read on a panel set on a wall of the tower of the Old Town Hall. The steeples of the local churches have witnessed all these and other events with no comment: the Baroque Old Town Church of St. Nicholas and Gothic Holy Týn Church. Originally there was a gold Hussite chalice on the gable of Týn Church. Since 1626 its gold has formed the halo of A Madonna. Symbols change, but vaults remain.

Old Town Square also brings the names of significant figures in Czech history to mind. King John of Luxembourg granted the old Town councillors the right to found a Town Hall with a stone tower in 1338. Here, in 1458, George of Poděbrady was elected king of Bohemia in the Diet. Since 1601 the Danish astronomer Tycho Brahe has laid at rest in oppositely situated Týn Church. In the house called „At the Golden Unicorn" (U zlatého jednorožce) on the corner of Železná Street the Czech composer Bedřich Smetana had a music school (1848) and Karel Havlíček Borovský, the founder of Czech modern journalism, also lived in it. And Franz Kafka, one of the most renowned world writers of Jewish culture, the German language and the Czech environment, was born on the other side, behind St. Nicholas's Church (1883). Czech, German and Jewish strata collectively formed the community of Prague and its culture for whole centuries.

Small Square (Malé náměstí), which hides behind the Old Town Hall, is also called Ryneček. It is triangular in shape and it is decorated with a Renaissance fountain (1560). Its narrow houses and arcades, recalling Romanesque and Gothic architects, create an intimate atmosphere. Old printing houses operated here (the Prague Bible, 1488) and the first pharmacies were established here on the basis of a royal permission. In the Middle Ages fruit was bought and sold here. In the past every Prague boy and craftsman knew where to get everything made of iron: at the shop called „At Rotts" (U Rotta) in Small Square. The shop was housed in a Neo-Renaissance building (1890). Its decoration was designed for an iron-mongery firm by Mikoláš Aleš, who along with Josef Mánes, the creator of the lunettes on the Prague horologe situated not far from here, represents romantic and folklore-inspired painting of the latter half of the 19th century. To be seen here is a picture documenting the fact that craft has a gold bottom and that rustic reason is the base of intelligence. It is Czech and comprehensible.

However, let us return to the very beginning – to the place where the Royal Route begins, i. e., to the Powder Tower. The rulers could not follow any other route but the Royal Route, because for eight-and-a-half centuries the centre of the Old Town was connected with the Castle by one bridge only. The first of them journeyed from their coronation in St. Vitus's Cathedral to the Old Town, where a solemn banquet took place by St. James Church. When in the 14th and 15th centuries they resided not at the Castle, but at the Royal Court, which stood on the site of the present Municipal House, they travelled to the Castle for their coronation in the opposite direction, but along the same route. When they travelled from Vienna for their coronation in Prague, they could set out from the Powder Gate for the Castle only along our route. The procession always waited for the ruler from Vienna in front of Poříčská Gate, situated in Karlín of the present. In those days it was still called Špitálské pole after a former hospital for persons with infectious diseases. In ancient times it was only a plain with the Růžodol summer palace. Otherwise there were only gardens, meadows and fields here. Karlín originated as Prague's oldest suburb as late as the 19th century and the noblemen, burghers and guilds of Prague's craftsmen assembled here under their banners. Some banners were so heavy that they had to be carried by eight men. The military captain stood at the head of the procession along with his people, these being followed by the gentry with their entourages, armour-bearers, trumpeters and drummers. Ladies of noble birth set in dozens of carriages. In one such procession there were 3391 horses and even four camels. The king was welcomed by the mayor at the head of the aldermen, who handed him the keys of the town. (Whole Karlín was almost destroyed by flooding in 2002.) On the boundary of the Little Quarter he was presented with the keys by the local people, the same procedure being repeated on the boundary of Hradčany. Solemn fanfares and cannon salves resounded simultaneously. These salves were omitted when Fridrich of the Palatinate arrived, because the king was frightened by cannon shots. The coronation processions of Maria Theresa in 1743, Leopold II in 1791 and Ferdinand V in 1836 were the most ostentatious. It is written that Ferdinand entered the Castle at the time when the procession was just forming by Poříčská Gate. The coronation processions are portrayed in the works of sketchers and engravers, who depicted not only the ceremonial proper, but also the changing appearance of Prague's towns. It suffices to take a glance at J. J. Dietzler's engraving of 1743 which with documentary faithfulness illustrates the route or the procession from the Powder Gate to St. Vitus's Cathedral.

The solemn welcoming ceremony took place by the Powder Gate. Let it be recalled that the foundation stone of the Powder Gate was laid in 1475 by King Vladislav Jagiello, the greater part of the structure being built by the bachelor of Týn School M. Rejsek. The gate was not specifically of military importance, being rather intended to beautify the neighbouring royal seat, the Royal Court. This is also documented by the windows on both its floors. The gate gained its name as late as the 17th century, when it served as a gunpowder storehouse. In 1823 a clock was placed on the tower, which in fact saved it from destruction when later the councillors had to decide the question of whether the delapidated tower should be demolished. The only argument against it was the usefulness of the tower clock.

In the past Celetná Street was by no means as quiet as it is nowadays. From 1901 to 1960 trams rattled their way along it. In the eighties of the 19th century horse-drawn carts and carriages passed this way, but even a long time previously the local inhabitants had complained about the noise made by the heavy carts and the shouting of street vendors. In 1862 the population of the upper part of Celetná Street submitted a complaint to the municipal authorities in which they stated that the noise in the street disturbed them. A special committee ascertained directly on the spot that in the course of one hour six goods carts, two fiacres and one post-office cart passed under the Powder Gate (in the transport peak) and admitted that the noise was really unbearable and directly harmful to human health. But what could it do?

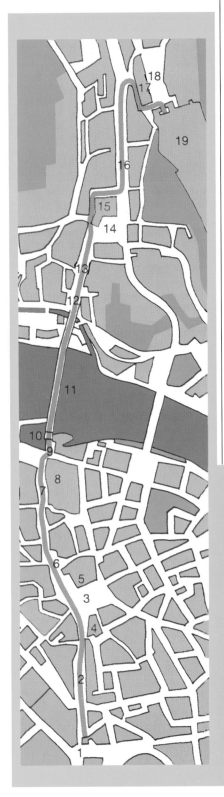

1 This self-portrait of the builder of the Powder Gate, **Matěj Rejsek,** is situated above the western gateway arch together with the emblem of the Old Town. It is surrounded by an inscription reading: „O burghers, do not permit evil people who live without inhibitions to do violence to me, a noble vessel."

2 The observation gallery below the hip roof of the Powder Gate is reached by means of 168 steps, but the view from this height is well worth of climbing them. The landmark shows the direction of the Royal Route, i. e., of Celetná Street, and the twin steeples of the Church of Our Lady of Týn, the steeples of St. Nicholas's Church in the Little Quarter, the tower of the Old Town Hall and Prague Castle on the horizon.

Plan of the royal route

1 Powder Gate
2 Celetná Street
3 Old Town Square
4 Church of Our Lady of Týn
5 Old Town Hall
6 Malé Square
7 Karlova Street
8 Clementinum
9 Křižovnické Square
10 Old Town Bridge
11 Charles Bridge
12 Little Quarter Bridge
13 Mostecká Street
14 Malostranské Square
15 St. Nicholas's Church
16 Nerudova Street
17 Ke Hradu
18 Hradčanské Square
19 Prague Castle

years younger. Not only the houses themselves, but also their names had different destinies.

6 The priests' house of **Týn Church** and the neighbouring house called **At the Three Kings** (U tří králů) have unique Gothic masonry up to their gables with rare stepped dentils. The writer F. Kafka lived in the house At the Three Kings from 1869 to 1907. The massive steeples of Týn Church rise above the priests' house.

7 The house called **At the Black Mother of God** (U černé Matky Boží) seemingly does not belong in this ancient street, but it has become a part of it to perfection. It represents Czech cubist architecture and originated in 1912, having been built by J. Gočár as the first building of its kind in Europe. The Baroque statue of the black Madonna dates in the 17th century.

3 The Powder Gate gained its present appearance in the years 1876 to 1892, when the uncompleted building of M. Rejsek was reconstructed in Neo-Gothic style by J. Mocker. His co-workers included a whole number of outstanding sculptors who hewed out ornamental decorations and the figures of men whose names were inscribed in the history of the Old Town. In the manner of the Old Town Bridge Tower the façade of the Powder Gate is divided into the individual zones of the cosmos – from the earthly to the heavenly one.

4–5 The houses called **At the White Peacock** (U bílého páva) and **At the Black Sun** (U černého slunce) differ at first glance: the Rococo façade with rich stucco decoration of the former originated about 1750, the latter, featuring the Classical style, being fifty

8

8 The right to found a Town Hall was granted to the Old Town by King John of Luxembourg in 1338. Shortly afterwards the construction of a tower was started next to the first Town Hall building. The Neo-Gothic wing of the Town Hall was destroyed by fire during the battles of 1945.

9 **The Master John Huss monument** was unveiled in 1915 and it is the work of L. Šaloun. The figure of John Huss is supplemented with a group of Hussites and emigrants of the period following the Battle of the White Mountain. They are gazing towards the place of execution of 1621.

10 **The Old Town astronomical clock** appeared on the tower already in the 15th century. It was built by Mikuláš of Kadaň and perfected by Hanuš of Růže. The upper astronomical sphere measures Central European and Old Czech time, which was counted from sunset. On its sides there are moving statues of a skeleton,

a Turk and a miser and an allegory of vanity. The lower calendarium is the work of J. Mánes and it bears allegories of the months and the signs of the Zodiac. On its sides can be seen the figures of a scribe, an astronomer, a chronicler and an angel. Above the upper sphere there is an angel with small windows behind which a procession of the Apostles takes place.

11–12 **The Gothic Church of Our Lady of Týn** was the town's chief church from Hussite times. Beneath the arched gables on the façade of Týn School there is a Venetian Renaissance painting The Assumption of Our Lady. Neighbouring Trčka's House was raised by one storey in the late 19th century at the cost of its former Late Baroque gables. Behind Týnská Street stands the house called At the Stone Bell (U kamenného zvonu), originally a Romanesque building of the 12th century which was later converted into a Gothic palace. Protruding into the square is Kinský Palace, a Late Baroque building which has rich Rococo stucco decorations. A grammar school, attended by F. Kafka, was once situated here.

13 The core of the house called **At the Minutes** (U minuty) is Gothic. It was reconstructed in the 16th century. The house gained its name At the Minutes not according to units of time, but after a tobacconist's shop with rapid sales.

10

9

built in the 15th century. It is called Kříž's House. Between the second and third houses of the Town Hall there was once a lane indicated by a passage with a number of uneven arcades. Kříž's House is characterized by a Renaissance window with a hemispherical tympanum. The windows on the second floor are Late Gothic and above them there are eighteen aldermen's coats-of-arms.

15 Malé Square originated in the Romanesque period. The front facing us is formed from the left by the house called In Paradise (V ráji), in which the botanist and courtier or Charles IV, Angelo of Florence, had a pharmacy in 1374. There were several pharmacies in this square where marzipan, the livers of wolves, dried frogs, remedies against a red nose and straightening devices for protruding ears were sold. Next to it is the house called At the White or the Blue Lion (U bílého lva or U modrého lva) with a Gothic portal and the oldest house sign in Prague. It has been preserved in its original place and it dates in 1400. In the 15th century there was a printing house here in which the first Bible printed in the Czech language originated. It was called The Prague Bible. Next in line is the house called At the Three White Roses (U tří bílých růží) or Rott's House (Rottův dům). Its façade features the Czech Renaissance style and it has paintings executed after cartoons by M. Aleš, who gained inspiration for the house sign from the Rožmberk roses in the frescos of the Town Hall at Prachatice. And he ranked first in something else too – it was in his house that the first flush toilet in Prague was installed.

16 We shall now leave Malé Square, make our way past the fountain with a Renaissance, manually hammered iron grille, and continue along the

14 The last backward view of Old Town Square, towards Týn Church. Why Týn? The word „týn" meant a raised, walled-in place – and indeed there was really once a hill here with a custom-house and also a fortified re-aloading centre for goods. The square itself was gradually levelled with deposits of earth up to several metres thick. The Old Town Hall is formed by a complex of buildings which were successively added to the core of the Town Hall. The oldest building is the one purchased by the community from the burgher Volflin od Kamene in 1338. Volflin's house has a portal of the 15th century and it is the main entrance to the Town Hall. The original core is adjoined by another Gothic house. It has a red façade and was

Royal Route, which now takes us through Karlova Street. This is a narrow, zig-zagging street and it is difficult to imagine than for centuries it was the most important artery in the town. It is even older that Charles Bridge. When the procession of Charles VI was to pass this way in 1723 the aldermen issued an order to the effect that all awnings, hanging signboards and craftsmen's shop signs were to be removed, because the street was too narrow even for the baldachin carried above the king. By the mouth of Karlova Street, on the left side, there is a sign in the form of a gold crown raised by two angels and directly in Karlova Street there is the sign of a gold crown with a cross on the same house. This house was called At the Golden Crown (U zlaté koruny), At the Little Black Horse (U černého koníčka), At the Carp (U kapra) – its names were often changed.

17 Standing on the corner of Jilská Street is a house called **At the Cats** (U Kočků). It is a top Baroque building on Romanesque foundations. At this point the Royal Route turns to the right.

18 In front of us there now appear the façades of the houses in **Husova Street**. Special mention should be made of the one called At the Black Snake (U černého hada), formerly named At the Golden Straw (U zlaté slámy).

19 Standing on the right in Husova Street is **Clam-Gallas Palace,** marked as the pearl of Baroque Prague. The palace façade is richly sculptured. On the ground-floor there are two massive portals with balconies supported by two giants – Heracles. Similarly as the sculptured decoration of the building as a whole they are the work of M. Braun and his workshop. M. Braun also created the relief decoration of the façade.

20 The relief fillings below the giants by the entrance to Clam-Gallas Palace are exceptionally valuable.

21 Turning off from Karlova Street at the place where it widens, from the house called At the Golden Well (U zlaté studně), is the bizarre little street called **Seminářská.**

22 Standing on the opposite side is the house **At the Blue Pike** (U modré štiky). In 1907 Dismas Slambor-Ponrepo opened Prague's first cinema here. In 1911 it was visited by T. A. Edison himself. It is alleged that he said: „Very nice, but small."

23 The whole of the right side of this part of Karlova Street is formed by the side façade of the **Clementinum,** now the State Library. Projecting from the end of the façade is the Italian Chapel (Vlašská kaple) of 1600, intended for the Italians living in Prague at that time, and also a wall of St. Clement's Church.

24 The house **At the Golden Well** (U zlaté studně) has an Early Baroque façade, its narrower front bearing stucco reliefs of the plague patrons St. Rochus and St. Sebastian.

25 The corner house facing us called **At the Golden Snake** (U zlatého hada). In 1714 it was purchased by an Armenian street coffee vendor by the name of Deotatus Damajan, who opened a coffee-house in it. At the same time he established a coffee-house in the Little Quarter house called At the Three Ostriches (U tří pštrosů) and it is still not known which of them was the first coffee-house in Prague.

26 In the house **At the Stone Mermaid** (U kamenné mořské panny) a mermaid was allegedly displayed and a great love story originated. Naturally, no one ever saw the mermaid.

27 **Pötting Palace** or **The Yellow House** has a Baroque façade with a portal by J. Santini. It was in the neighbouring house that the renowned astronomer J. Kepler completed his work Astronomia nova and it was here that he also discovered his first two laws on the movement of the planets.

28 Karlova Street is closed on the left side by **Coloredo-Mansfeld Palace** with a conspicuous portal bearing the family coat-of-arms.

ÚSTŘEDÍ ČS UNITÁŘŮ

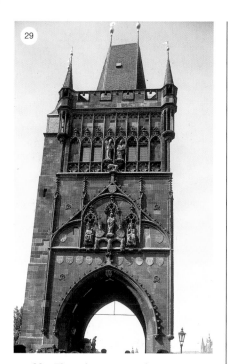

29 The dominant of Křižovnické Square is the **Old Town Bridge Tower.** It originated after a design by the builder of St. Vitus's Cathedral, Peter Parler, in the 14th century. The eastern façade, divided up by cornices, bears witness to the medieval idea about the composition of the universe: the lowest position is occupied by the earthly zone, higher up is the lunar sphere and above it in the solar sphere there are sculptures of Charles IV and Václav IV between which there stands on a symbol of the bridge its patron St. Vitus. Situated in the highest place is the stellar sphere with statues of the Czech patrons.

30 Under the lower cornice there are scenes from sinful life on Earth, often with naturalistic details.

31 In 1848 **a statue of Charles IV** with allegorical figures of the four faculties and the king's contemporaries was placed in the centre of the square.

32 **The Church of the Holy Saviour** is in essence Renaissance with Baroque alterations and supplements.

33 Standing on the right side of the square is the monastery of the Knights of the Cross with a Red Star and the Church of St. Francis Seraphinicus. The order of Knights with a Red Star had the right to collect duty on the bridge and they cared for the safety of the bridge with the money they gained.

34 On the corner of St. Francis Church stands a **vinicultural column with St. Wenceslas,** the patron of vintners. Beneath the column is the

oldest town paving in Prague. It was transferred here from Judith's Bridge.

35 **Křižovnické Square** originated in its present form as late as 1848, when a statue of Charles IV stood here. At that time the embankment arch of Judith's Bridge was also covered.

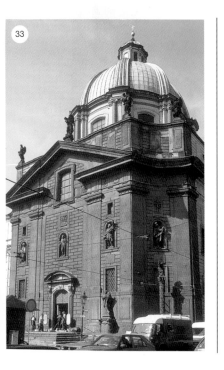

CHARLES BRIDGE

When the flood waters of the River Vltava caused Judith's Bridge to collapse in 1342 the town could not remain lone without a connection between the two banks. And so on 9 July, 1357 the Emperor Charles IV laid the foundation stone of a new bridge, initially called the Stone Bridge, then the Prague Bridee and from 1780 Charles Bridge after its founder. The time of the foundation of the bridge was not a matter of chance and thus we know it precisely down to the minute. It was determined not only by astronomy, but also by numeral magic – the ascending and descending order of me odd numbers: 1–3–5–7–9–7–5–3–1. The favourable constellation of the planets naturally also played a role. The first four numbers indicate the years – 1357, the figure 9 indicates the day, 7 the month, 5 the hour and 31 the minutes. Thus 9. 7. 1357 at 5. 31. The statues and arcades above the main cornice of the Old Town Bridge Tower are framed by a large triangular gable on which there are 24 decorations, so-called crabs - the astronomical symbol of the solar sphere. On the Gothic arch of the gateway there are 28 of them indicating the lunar sphere. And there are many more similar astronomical mathematical symbols here.

Portrayed on the façade of the Old Town Bridge Tower and on the vault of its gateway is a kingfisher in the centre of a linenfold. A legend says that it is a reminder of the female barber Zuzana, who once saved King Václav IV. However, the truth is different – kingfishers were the favourite symbol of the king's wife Žofie. The kingfisher is known from Greek legends: it was the symbol of a faithful wife, domestic peace and feminine beauty and only later did it become the symbol of barbers. The Old Town Bridge Tower conceals also other picture-puzzles. Two mysterious inscriptions were discovered in the past beneath its original roof: Signatesignatemeremetangisetangis and Romatibisubitomotibusibitamor. They are written in a circle and they read the same whether you start at the beginning or the end. They were common medieval magic spells which were intended to protect a building. The translation of the first Latin inscription reads as follows: Remember, beware and guard yourself; the moment you touch me you will die. The other inscription means: Through reversals love will be sacrificed to you. And another surprise is concealed in the interior of the tower: on the top of the winding staircase there is a sculpture of a prisoner – a hunchback whose conception ranks it beyond its time (it dates in the period of Peter Parler). It is a striking reminder of Quasimodo in Notre Dame in Paris.

The construction of the bridge was supervised by P. Parler, then twenty-four years of age. The bottom of the Vltava was too deep below the surface and there was firm rock at a depth of up to nine metres so the piers of the bridge were built on grillage made from oak wood and millstones. Parler had to avoid the remainders of Judith's Bridge and furthermore there was the bridge tower in the Little Quarter, situated towards the course of Judith's Bridge. He solved both problems in an ingenious way: he made use of the old Little Quarter Bridge Tower in the new structure and deflected the bridge in a curve. The bridge was consecrated to St. Vitus, a statue of whom is situated in the middle of the eastern façade on a double arched model of the bridge. The history of Bohemia passed over Charles Bridge. Both the coronation and the burial processions of the kings crossed it. The

36 Aerial view of Charles Bridge, part of the Little Quarter and Prague Castle. At the right end of the white ribbon of the Old Town Weir – the oldest weir in Prague – is the Novotný Footbridge with the tower of the former Old Town Waterworks. The glowing white building on the opposeite bank is Lichtenštejn Palace. Situated at the end of Charles Bridge are the two Little Quarter Bridge Towers behind which the Royal Route continues along Mostecká Street to Malostranské Square and below the steeple of St. Nicholas's Church. Prague Castle is just as monumental when viewed from a height as when seen from Charles Bridge.

heads of the Czech lords executed in 1621 in Old Town Square were hung from the battlements of the Old Town Bridge Tower and remained there for ten whole years.

In 1413 Master John Huss hung his passionate protest against the selling of indulgences on the bridge tower. In the 15th century the Hussites waged battle here, in 1611 Passau troops tried to penetrate into the Old Town here and in 1648 students fought here in the ranks of the defenders of the Old Town against the Swedes. In 1848 barricades again stood on the bridge and once again students helped to build them. To commemorate the year 1648 a statue of a student – the only one in Prague – was placed in the courtyard of the nearby Clementinum.

Until 1816 a bridge-toll was collected for everything on Charles Bridge: for wine, for a horse and even for a bride.

For a long time the new bridge existed without the decoration which is now so typical of it. Raised on it first of all in accordance with a medieval custom was a cross with The Crucified. The main part of the Baroque decoration originated from 1706 to 1714, when thirty statues and groups of statues were set in place on the bridge. Most of them came from the workshops of leading Baroque masters – M. Braun and J. Brokoff and his sons. The oldest statue on the bridge, St. John Nepomuk of 1683, is the work of J. Brokoff the Elder. The last group of statues appeared on the bridge in 1928 – it portrays Cyril and Method and is the work of K. Dvorak.

Dishonest tradesmen, especially bakers, were lowered into the Vltava in a cage from the fifth pier, on which there is a statue Pieta.

Charles Bridge was the victim of numerous floods, the first occurring during its construction and the second in 1432, when the water caused five piers to collapse. However, after the elapse of only four years a grand tournament took place on the bridge. During the flood of 1890 the water rose by four metres and the accumulated timber demolished the bridge again, three piers collapsing this time, taking two of Brokoff's groups of statues with them. The repair work took years to complete, but this time the piers were rooted in the rock base.

Charles Bridge continues to Kampa Island by the Little Quarter river bank, from which it is separated by the so-called Devil's Stream. The oldest report about Kampa dates in 1169. Kampa originated as the result of the artificial hollowing-out of a drive for the conducting of water to the Grand Prior Mills. It became a real island in the 16th century, when its level was raised by means of deposits from the remainders of the houses destroyed by fire in the Little Quarter in 1541. In those days there were no steps leading to the bridge as there are today and so when a flood occurred people had to use a ladder to climb on to the bridge. A wooden flight of steps existed here from 1785, replaced in 1844 by a stone one. From 1798 to 1804 the linguist, historian and revivalist „blue abbot" Josef Dobrovský lived on Kampa. The painter Jiří Trnka, the illustrator of the novel Grand-mother (Babička), Adolf Kašpar, the historian of Prague, Zdeněk Wirth and the actors Jan Werich and Eduard Kohout lived on the island. Pottery markets, which had formerly taken place in Pohořelec, were transferred to the square in the late 16th century and still take place every year.

For a long time Charles Bridge remained in darkness after dusk and pedestrians were obliged to carry torches. Proof of this lies in an order of 1763 according to which torches had to be extinguished on the balustrade of the bridge above Kampa so that fires did not break out in the houses below the bridge.

Standing in front of the Little Quarter Bridge Towers forming the end of Charles Bridge is the building of the former Little Quarter customs house. It was built in Renaissance style in the late 16th century and originally also had Renaissance gables. In the building adjoining the smaller bridge tower there is a votive relief of the latter half of the 12th century which is a valu-able monument of Romanesque sculpture.

However, in the 19th century the relief was damaged and consequently we do not know the identity of the ruler on the throne and the kneeling young man. Most likely the Emperor Friedrich Barbarosa is bestowing the royal title on Prince Vladislav II, which happened in Regensburg in 1158, or perhaps Vladislav is presenting the people of Prague with the just finished bridge. The smaller Little Quarter Bridge Tower is Romanesque and dates in the mid-12th century. It was later subjected to Renaissance alterations. The higher tower was built at the time of George of Poděbrady in 1464. When you pass between the two towers take note of the deep grooves in the stones situated quite high above your head on the left side. They are the work of the halberd guards of the Little Quarter who became bored when keeping watch.

The Little Quarter Bridge Towers were the main parts of the fortifications of the Little Quarter. The higher tower has an architectural scheme similar to that of the Old Town Bridge Tower, but it has no sculptured decoration even though there are recesses for statues on it. The lower bridge tower, whose core is Romanesque, is a remainder of the fortifications and although it is older than Judith's Bridge it was linked with it in its way. The higher tower has never had a gateway. Its gallery is accessible and a unique view to the west of the Little Quarter and Hradčany and to the east of the Old Town can be obtained from it. The gate between the two towers bears the Luxembourg emblem of a lioness, the Czech lion with two tails and the Moravian eagle. The Old Town emblems visible beneath the gargoyle were placed here later.

The appearance of Charles Bridge changed in the course of the long centuries. Historians tell us that the eastern part of the Old Town Bridge Tower documents the idea of medieval Man concerning the composition of the universe and that the whole tower is perhaps the arch of triumph of Charles IV. Some of the statues and groups of statues also have their own destiny. The old statue of George of Poděbrady which stood on the bridge from his times disappeared similarly as another statue of George, an equestrian one, which was situated on the third pier. Balbin brings to mind the fact that once a statue of justice, a column with a lion, a wayside column and a crucifix were situated on the bridge. Floods destroyed the original statue of a knight with the emblem of the Old Town which, similarly as elsewhere in Europe, was the symbol of the bridge right of the knight Roland. Later he was called Bruncvík after the legend about a knight with a lion. However, the original Bruncvík was deprived of his head during the Thirty Years War and in 1884 he was replaced with a new statue – only the pedestal of the old one remained. After a time Brokoff's older Pieta of 1695 to 1698 was transferred to the Pod Petřínem Hospital, the statue of St. Ludmilla with the small Václav being moved to the centre of the bridge from the ramp of Prague Castle. After the flood of 1890 bridge piers collapsed together with a group of statues of St. Francis Xavier and a group of statues of St. Ignatius, which after a time were replaced with the missionaries Cyril and Method. St. Francis Xavier returned to the bridge in a precise copy together with a self-portrait of the young M. Brokoff in the upper part of the group of statues. Very few people now know that until the flood of 1785 there was a small island with the saint's chapel in the river below the statue of St. John of Nepomuk.

The most popular group of statues on Charles Bridge is definitely the group with St. John de Matha, St. Felix de Valois and the hermit St. Ivan. Captive Christians behind a prison grille are guarded by the renowned figure of a Turk with scourges. In the 19th century the citizens of Prague were fond of betting how many buttons the Turk had. The saying „You stand like the Turk on Charles Bridge" also originated at that time.

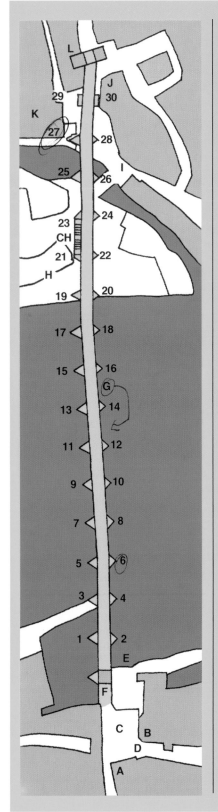

Plan of Charles Bridge

1. The group of statues of It. Ives
2. The Madonna with St. Bernard
3. The group of statues of St. Barbara, St. Margaret and St. Elizabeth
4. The Madonna, St. Dominic and St. Thomas Aquinus
5. The group of statues Pieta
6. The statue of the Holy Cross
7. The statue of St. Joseph
8. The statue of St. Anne
9. St. Francis Xavier baptising an Indian, a Red Indian, a Negro, a Tatar and a Japanese
10. St. Cyril and Method
11. St. Christopher
12. St. John the Baptist
13. The statue of St. Francis Borgia
14. St. Norbert, St. Wenceslas and St. Sigismund
15. St. Ludmilla with Václav
16. St. John Nepomuk
17. St. Francis Seraphicus
18. St. Anthony of Padua, a preacher
19. The group of statues of St. Vincent Ferrarius and St. Procopius
20. The apostle St. Jude Thaddeus
21. St. Nicholas of Tolentino
22. The statue of St. Augustine
23. St. Luitgarde and Christ
24. The statue of St. Cajetanus
25. St. Adalbert, the first Czech bishop
26. Philip Benicius, the father of the Servites
27. St. John de Matha and St. Felix de Valois with St. Ivan. The prisoners with the Christians guarded by a Turk
28. St. Vitus on a rock with a lion
29. The statue of St. Wenceslas
30. The statue of the Holy Saviour with St. Cosmas and St. Damian

A. The Church of the Holy Saviour
B. The Church of St. Francis Seraphinus
C. The statue of Charles IV
D. The vinicultural column
E. The head of Bradac
F. The Old Town Bridge Tower
G. The cross set in the balustrade
H. The house At the Painting of Our Lady (U obrázku Panny Marie)
CH. The flight of steps on Kampa
I. The Devil's Stream with the Prague Venice
J. The house At the Three Ostriches
K. The Grand Prior Mill
L. The Little Quarter Bridge Tower

37 About five metres to the north of **Charles Bridge** there once stood Judith's Bridge, its stone predecessor. King Vladislav II had it built after the catastrophe of the wooden bridge. It is alleged that the king's consort Judith, after whom the bridge was named, kept a watch on the construction work. It was 514 metres long and 7 metres wide and it had 21 arches. For the sake of comparison let it be mentioned that Charles Bridge is 516 metres long, nearly 10 metres wide and it has 16 piers. The two towers of Judith's Bridge still partly exist – on the Little Quarter side it is the smaller of the two bridge towers there and on the Old Town side the other tower is walled-up in the projection of the monastery of the Knights of the Cross.

38 Still to on the area in front of Křižovnické Square can be seen the preserved end arch of Judith's Bridge on which there was the stone head of **Bradáč**, serving the people of Prague as a sign of warning against floods. In 1840 it was transferred to the right embankment wall.

39

39 Standing on the right side of the bridge is a group of statues **The Holy Cross and Calvary** (6). The cross stood here already in the 14th century, when the bridge was still without statues.

40 Perhaps the best-known is the group of statues of **John de Matha and Felix de Valois,** who redeemed captured Christians from the Turks – hence the Turk keeping guard. St. Ivan supplements the two Trinitarians. The group of statues dates in 1714 and it is the work of F. M. Brokoff.

41 Several centuries separate the Little Quarter Bridge Towers from the two steeples of St. Nicholas's Church. The cellars of the houses on the right side of the bridge contain the foundations of the piers of old Judith's Bridge.

42 Set in the balustrade of the bridge on the right side, between the statues of John the Baptist (12) and St. Norbert (14), is a two-armed cross which marks the place were John of Nepomuk was allegedly thrown into the river. The belief reigned in Prague that if a person placed his hand on the cross and made a wish, the wish would come true.

43 The group of statues of **St. Luitgarde** (23) by M. B. Braun of 1710 is the essence of the Prague Baroque and the most beautiful sculpture on the bridge. In a mystic vision St. Luitgarde is exchanging hearts with Christ.

44 The Devil's Stream (Čertovka) was originally the drive of mills. In the 16th century it was called Rožmberk's Ditch after Vilém of Rožmberk. It acquired its present name in the 19th century. The part on the right is called the Prague Venice.

45 Since the 16th century a statue of a knight has stood on the left pier on Kampa Island. It is called **Bruncvík.** The statue represented a confirmation of the right of the Old Town to a bridge and to the duties from goods transported across it.

40

41

42

43

44

45

THE ROYAL ROUTE IN THE LITTLE QUARTER

From Mostecká Street the Royal Route continues to Malostranské Square, first simply called Rynek (Square). Its landmark is formed by the green dome and the belfry or St. Nicholas's Church, the most outstanding building of the Prague Baroque of the early 18th century. It is the work of two Dienzenhofers, father and son. The church together with the house of the Jesuits divides the square into two different parts. From the 16th century the upper part was called Italian Square after the shops of Italian merchants and from 1844 it was called Štěpanské Square. From 1858 the lower part was called Radecké Square, but that was not its official name. From the 14th to the 18th century butchers' shops were situated here and until 1782 there was also a pillory here. From 1859 to 1918 a bronze monument commemorating Marshal Radecký, cast from looted Sardinian works and weighing ten tons, stood on the site of a former fountain in the middle of the lower area. The bronze monument of Ernest Denis, which from 1928 to 1940 stood in front of the façade of the present Malostranské Cafe, also disappeared. Not until 1869 did the two parts gain the name Malostranské Square.

On the site of the former butchers' shops several houses originated in front of St. Nicholas's Church which were connected in the Rococo building called At the Stone Table (U kamenného stolu) in which the Malostranská Cafe is situated. Standing on the corner of the eastern side of the square is the Late Renaissance building of the former Little Quarter Town Hall. Opposite it, on the northern side, there is the front of several palaces, of which Smiřský Palace and Šternberk Palace are particularly noteworthy. In 1541 a great fire broke out here which destroyed the grater part of the Little Quarter and heavily damaged Hradčany and Prague Castle.

As the royal processions continued they crossed the mouth of Karmelitská Street, through which the main communication with the south of the country led, and headed for St. Nicholas's Church. On the left side there is a number of interesting houses. The last one with arcading, called The Golden Lion (Zlatý lev), is now the only purely Renaissance building in the whole square.

The whole of the western side of the square opposite St. Nicholas's Church is taken up by Lichtenštejn Palace, which originated in the late 18th century as the result of the reconstruction of five Renaissance buildings. From 1620 to 1627 the governor Karel of Lichtenštejn, the originator of the execution of Czech lords in Old Town Square in 1521, lived in it. From 1848 the palace was the seat of the provincial military headquarters. Two days after the proclamation of the independence of the Czechoslovak Republic on 28 October, 1918 the commanding general Pavel Kostřánek had notices about martial law printed and prepared arrests and executions. The Czech naval battery and the Adriatic flotillas placed machine guns in front of the palace and the general capitulated. The naval battery consisted of sailors who were just on leave or in hospital and the whole action was the only military intervention of the Czech navy during World War I.

A statue The Holiest Trinity, created in 1715 after a design by G. B. Alliprandi and expressing gratitude for the end of the plague epidemic, stands in front of the palace. The plague claimed 12.000 victims in two years. However, at that time the town was not very concerned with cleanliness – it was written in 1604 that in Malostranské Square there were such large piles of rubbish that „passers-by and other useless people have their lairs here". All that remains to say is that in 1604 no royal procession took place and that the Emperor Rudolph II had other problems to cope with.

From the upper part of Malostranské Square, directly from thc corner of Lichtenštejn Palace, the Royal Route continues through steep Nerudova

Street. Narrow Zámecká Lane opposite the corner of the palace would lead us to the Castle Steps (Zámecké schody), which rise to Hradčanské Square. The steps are called the New Castle Steps (Nové zámecké schody), but one of the paradoxes of history lies in the fact that they are older than the Old Castle Steps (Staré zámecké schody) running from the Castle to Klárov.

For whole centuries Nerudova Street was the main communication leading to Prague Castle. In the place where it narrows sharply in the middle of its length there stood still in the 18th century a drawbridge with a ditch. The Little Quarter came to an end at this spot.

Nerudova Street was named after the poet and journalist Jan Neruda who lived here in the house called At the Two Suns (U dvou slunců) and in his works described not only the picturesque environment of the Little Quarter, but also and mainly me destinies of its people.

The lower part of the street is rather of a palace character. Apart from Morzini and Thun-Hohenštejn Palaces the Church of Our Lady of the Theatines with a former monastery is situated here. In 1834 J. K. Tyl established a theatre in its refectory.

The upper part of the street is mainly lined with burghers' houses. The artistic appearance of the palaces and burghers' houses was determined by the High Baroque, which provided their gables, portal and facades with fine stucco decoration and mostly covered their former Renaissance appearance. However, even so elements of the Renaissance and old Gothic cellarage exist here and on Janský Hill the remainders of a Romanesque rotunda have been discovered.

The street is very steep and it is interesting to note the way in which old architects solved the problem of the upper line of the houses, roofs and gables in order that the street might form a whole. Most of the houses have a striking house sign ranking among the most beautiful in Prague. Those who are able to use their eyes will notice also their stucco decorations and the details of the door handles, grille gates and balconies and the composition of the windows on the individual floors – this was another problem with which the steep street confronted architects. At the turn of the 19th and 20th centuries the question arose of whether a rack railway should lead through the street, but it was finally dismissed.

From 1683 the royal processions continued up to the Castle by means of the newly built Castle ramp, called Ke Hradu, which shortened the journey. Until then the shortest way of access from the Little Quarter to the Castle was via the New Castle Steps, which meant a breakneck path for pedestrians and riders alike. Thus the royal processions continued from Nerudova Street by means of a long detour running through equally steep Úvoz, formerly called The Deep Path (Hluboká cesta), as far as Pohořelec. For centuries that was the main way of access to the Castle. Below the gate of Strahov Monastery the processions turned round and continued through present Loretánská Street to Hradčanské Square and finally to the Castle.

However, the detour via Úvoz, Pohořelec and Loretánská Street is not regarded as a part of the Royal Route now.

At the time of a coronation an enormous podium stood in front of the Castle in Hradčanské Square on which the ruler was welcomed when entering the territory of Hradčany and Prague Castle. The grille gates of the Castle, which since the time of Rudolph II have been decorated with statues of giants by I. F. Platzer, afforded the procession access to the cour d'honneur. It then proceeded through the Matthias Gate to St. Vitus's Cathedral, in which the solemn coronation ceremony took place. Twenty kings of five dynasties received the Czech crown here and it is here that the Royal Route comes to an end.

46

47

48

46 The last backward view from the Little Quarter Bridge towers brings whole centuries into confrontation – from the Gothic up to the present, represented by the television transmitter in Žižkov. The western façade of the Old Town Bridge Tower is quite conspicuously poorer than the eastern one: its original decoration was destroyed by the artillery fire of the Swedes who attacked the Old Town from across the bridge in 1648.

47 When gazing from the Little Quarter Bridge Towers to the west we see another part of the Royal Route, continuing through Mostecká Street to Malostranské Square. The landmarks in this view are the steeples of St. Nicholas's Church and Prague Castle. Seen on the horizon are the steeples of Strahov Monastery.

48 The right front of Mostecká Street is formed by a row of houses which sprang up on the site of a medieval bishop's court. From the 14th century it was also occupied for some time by the archbishops, but in 1419, during the Hussite wars, it was destroyed by fire. The Renaissance, High Baroque and Classical styles mingle on the facades of the houses.

49 **Kaunicz Palace** originated as the result of the reconstruction of Renaissance burghers' houses in the 18th century and it represents the transition from the Rococo to the Classical style. Its sculptured decoration is the work of I. F. Platzer's workshop. The magnificence of the central portal reveals itself in the full extent when viewed from a distance – from oppositely situated Josefská Street.

50 In Malostranské Square we pass between two houses. On the left the one called At the Petržílkas (U Petržílků), which is one of the oldest houses in the Little Quarter in general. It has a corner oriel and the remainders of a fortification tower from the time of Přemysl II have been preserved on its area. The whole of the southern side of Malostranské Square is practically wholly lined with old burghers' houses. Still standing on the right is the pseudo-Renaissance building of the former Little Quarter Credit Bank, which originated from three already standing Baroque houses with arcades and gables.

49

50

51 To be seen on the eastern side of Malostranské Square is Kaiserštejn Palace, a Baroque building with an Early Classical façade.

52 From 1908 to 1914 the world-renowned opera singer **Ema Destinnová** lived in Kaiserštejn Palace, a fact brought to mind by a memorial tablet and a bust of the singer on the façade.

53 On the corner formed by the square and Letenská Street stands the former **Little Quarter Town Hall.** The entrance from the arcade is decorated with the Little Quarter emblem of 1660.

54 In the immediate neighbourhood the lens of the camera captured the green steeple of St. Vitus's Cathedral at the Castle and the dark turret of the corner oriel of Renaissance **Smiřický Palace**. In 1618 the palace was the centre of the preparations of the uprising of the Estates and it was here that the event called the Prague defenestration, was decided.

55 The landmark of Malostranské Square is formed by the **steeples of Baroque St. Nicholas's Church.** The slender steeple of the belfry did not belong to the Jesuits, who had the church built, but to the community, which provided the belfry with the emblem of the Little Quarter, equipped it with bells and also used it as its watch-tower. The historic tram in the foreground is now only a tourist attraction running through the streets of the Little Quarter and the Old Town.

ZDE ŽILA   EMA DESTI

55

17 17

17 HOLEŠOVICE
PELC TYROLKA

56 From the 16th century the upper part of Malostranské Square was called Italian Square (Vlašský rynek) after the adjoining colony of Italian builders, merchants and craftsmen. Standing in front of Lichtenštejn Palace is a **columnwith a group of statues The Holiest Trinity,** raised here after a design by G. B. Alliprandi in 1715 as an expression of gratitude for the end of the plague epidemy.

57 The whole side of the upper part of the square opposite St. Nicholas's Church is taken up by **Lichtenštejn Palace.** From 1620 to 1627 it was the seat of „the bloody governor" Karel of Lichtenštejn, marked as the originator of the execution of the Czech lords in Old Town Square after the Battle of the White Mountain. In the 18th century the only collecting place of letters in the whole of Prague was situated here. Letter-boxes did not exist in those days, but letters could be handed over to postmen who walked through the street with rattles.

58 The most outstanding artists of their time participated in the decoration of the interior of St. Nicholas's Church. In the dome there is a fresco **The Celebration of the Holiest Trinity** by F. X. Balko. The vault of the nave is decorated with a fresco The Celebration of St. Nicholas by J. L. Kracker. Situated on pillars beneath the dome are four huge statues of church fathers by I. F. Platzer, who also sculptured the statue of St. Nicholas on the high altar and most of the altar sculptures. The church organ dates in the mid-18th century and W. A. Mozart also payed on it.

59 The huge building of **St. Nicholas's Church** originated in the first half of the 18th century on the area of an old Gothic church which had occupied the area since the 13th century. The presbytery with a cupola and a typical copper roof above it are the work of K. I. Dienzenhofer. His son completed the work which his father K. Dienzenhofer had started on the building nearly fifty years earlier. The slender steeple of the belfry was constructed a little later next to Dienzenhofer's cupola by A. Lurago.

60

60 Behind Lichtenštejn Palace the Royal Route continues from upper Malostranské Square and passes through Nerudova Street. Standing on the corner on its right side is the house called **Atthe Black Eagle** (U černého orla) or **At the Cat** (U kocoura). The little street running alongside the house would take us to the New Castle Steps leading to the Castle.

61 Situated on the left side of the street is **Morzin Palace** of 1714. It has two portals and the balustrade of its balcony is borne by the statues of two Moors – an emblem from the coat-of-arms of the Morzin family. Count Václav Morzin fought against the Moors.

62 The sign in the form of a gold goblet on house No. 16 was set in place in 1660 by a goldsmith by the name of B. Schumann, who owned the building.

63 The sculptures **Day and Night,** the statues of Moors and the allegories of the four parts of the world on the attic of Morzin Palace are the work of F. M. Brokoff.

64 High Baroque Thun Palace, or formerly Kolowrat Palace, also bears the symbol of the family in the form of sculptures of two huge eagles on the large portal.

65–70 Signs on houses in Nerudova Street. The sign on the house called At the Three Fiddles (U tří housliček) brings three generations of the Edlinger family of violin-builders to mind. House No. 28 has a sign in the form of a gold wheel. On house No. 27 there is a gold key. There are fourteen house signs with a key in Prague – a key meant safety. On house No. 41 there is a relief of a red lion holding a cup in its paws – the symbol of goldsmiths. Jan Neruda lived, in the house named At the Two Suns (U dvou slunců) whose relief sign dates in 1730. The neighbouring house, has a rich Baroque relief of a white swan in its sign.

61

62

63

67

64

68

65

69

66

70

71 The end of the right side of Neruda Street is formed by two houses – **At the Three Black Eagles** (U tří černých orlů) and **At the Three Red Crosses** (U tří červených křížků). Rising high above their dormer windows and above Radnické Steps in Schwarzenberg or Lobkovitz Palace, which has a graffiti-decorated façade after Venetian models and which is a typical

sample of the Czech Renaissance combining the Italian conception with the home tradition.

72 The Radnické Steps (Radnické schody) are situated between the house At the Golden Star (U zlaté hvězdy), whose façade closes Nerudova Street, and the communication called Ke Hradu. They lead to Loretánská Street. Their foot is lined by

two statues – St. John Nepomuk by M. J. Brokoff of 1709 and St. Joseph by an unknown sculptor of 1714.

73 The street Ke Hradu was hewn out in rock in the 17th century.

74 Before the origin of Ke Hradu, which shortened the route, the royal processions made their way towards Hradčanské Square via Úvoz and Pohořelec. The continuation of Nerudova Street was called Deep Path (Hluboká cesta).

75 The most conspicuous building in this part of Úvoz is the barocized house called At the Stone Column (U kamenného sloupu).

76 The neighbouring house At the Golden Apple (U zlatého jablka) has a Baroque statue of Our Lady in a corner recess.

III. STRAHOV, POHOŘELEC, HRADČANY

In 1140 Prince Vladislav II and the Olomouc bishop Jindřich Zdík founded a Premonstratensian monastery at Strahov. Due to its size it surpassed even the seat of the sovereign at Prague Castle. It is unquestionably the biggest Czech Romanesque building which perhaps had no like in the neighbouring countries in the 12th century in view of its size. It is most likely that it was built by the prince's workshop simultaneously engaged in the construction of Prague Castle and its fortifications. This is witnessed by the choice of the building site in the place where it entered the Prague valley, where a deep forest ended and where there was a plain which had always had to be guarded, because the seat of the princes was the most vulnerable from this side. Strahov Monastery was thus fortified, also being intended to secure the protection of Prague Castle.

The first abbot of Strahov Monastery was a certain Gezo, a former canon from Cologne-on-Rhine. He arrived at Strahov in 1143 and the monastery and the church were probably completed during his lifetime because in 1150 Bishop Zdík as well as Queen Gertruda and her consort, King Vladislav II, were buried here.

The ostentatious building of the monastery was the destination of many important delegations to Prague and the monastery refectory served as the Diet until the time of Přemysl Otakar II, i. e., to the latter half of the 13th century. In 1258 the monastery was destroyed by fire due to the carelessness of one of the monks, but it was renewed and newly modified in the space of five years. The Renaissance and the Baroque required comfort warmed by sunshine and so the interior of Strahov Monastery also changed. At that time the remains of the founder of the Premonstratensian order, St. Norbert, were also transferred to Strahov.

For whole centuries Strahov Monastery was considered to be a work of the 16th and especially the 17th century. A report of a direct participant in the Hussite wars, the author of the Hussite Chronicle, Vavřinec of Březová, stating that the monastery was wholly destroyed by the Hussites in 1420 was handed down for a long time. The inaccuracy of this information was proved by archeological research carried out from 1950. It discovered that for a long time a Baroque mantle covered the most important parts of the ground-floor of the old Romanesque monastery-its chapter hall, refectory and out-buildings.

The abbot's Church of the Assumption of Our Lady, originally a triple-naved basilica of the 12th century, was rebuilt several times, extensively for the last time in 1601. At the cost of the Emperor Rudolph II and as thanks for the end of the plague the Church of St. Rochus, a remarkable combination of the Gothic and the Renaissance, was built in the Strahov courtyard on that occasion. The Church of the Assumption of Our Lady gained its present appearance as late as in the mid-18th century. Since then it has had a decorated Baroque vault covered with magnificent stucco cartouches. The new Baroque façade of the church arid the steeple date in the mid-18th century. They were built by A. M. Lurago of Italy.

During the reconstruction of the monastery in the seventies of the 17th century G. D. Orsi built the beautiful Theological Hall of Strahov Monastery and in the same period he built a large extension and enlarged the whole monastery after a project by the French architect J. B. Mathey.

77   View from Strahov towards Prague Castle. In the foreground on the right is Strahov Monastery with the Premonstratensian Church of Our Lady and visible in the background is Prague Castle with St. Vitus's Cathedral. The three steeples of the Loretto are visible by the left edge of the photo. Amid the greenery in the left upper corner is the royal Belvedere summer palace and lying in front of the Castle ◄   is Hradčany with the suburb of Pohořelec.

The Baroque entrance gate, decorated with a statue of St. Norbert, dates in 1742. The complicated building development of Strahov Monastery was ended, its Baroque period being crowned by the Classical building of the library, a work of the prominent Prague architect J. I. Palliardi.

The Strahov library ranks among the oldest and the most valuable of Czech libraries. Its beginnings date back to the Baroque period, but this does not mean that its history begins there. The Baroque book collection is the fourth in order formed at Premonstratensian Strahov and also the first to be preserved in its whole. Only the torsos of the three preceding Romanesque, Gothic and Renaissance collections have remained. If the Theological Hall is beautiful, then the Philosophical Hall is even more so. It covers the height of two floors and its vault is decorated with frescos by the Viennese painter F. A. Maulbertsch. In the centre of the monastery's Court of Paradise there is a pool into which one of Prague's first water mains led. The size of the cloisters on three sides of the monastery building affords an idea of the magnitude of the monastery at the time of its foundation.

In 1375 the vice-burgrave Aleš of Malíkovice founded a community below Strahov which in later years was called Pohořelec after the frequent fires which occurred there (hořet = to burn). The Strahov gateway affording access to Břevnov, Strahov and Bílá hora stood by Pohořelec Square. However, until the early 14th century there was a deep forest here which reached to the western gate of Prague Castle. Hunts often took place there. A road to north-west Bohemia ran through the forest. In 1310 this place became a battlefield where the troops of Jindřich of Lípa and Vítek of Landštejn forced back the soldiers of King Henry of Carinthia. After his defeat he and his whole court secretly left Prague Castle and fled to Bavaria. John of Luxembourg then succeeded to the Czech throne. During his reign the tributary town of Hradčany was founded on the initiative of the Castle burgrave Hynek Berka of Dubá. It spread out on a long ridge demarcated in the south by the slope above the Little Quarter and in the north by Stag Ditch and the River Brusnice, i. e., approximately round present Hradčanské Square.

Charles IV enlarged the territory of Hradčany by attaching Pohořelec, Loretánské Square and Nový Svět (New World) to it. He then had the whole town fortified, Strahov Monastery and a part of Petřín being incorporated into the new fortifications. In spite of this Hradčany remained Prague's smallest town. During the siege of the Táborites in 1420 it was practically wholly burned to ashes. It experienced its greatest tragedy in 1541 when it was completely destroyed by fire. The newly built parts featured the Renaissance. From the Sixties of the 16th century the Czech aristocracy began to build a number of Renaissance palaces and the importance of Hradčany, raised to a royal town by the Emperor Rudolph II, rose. After the Battle of the White Mountain (1620) the Hradčany burghers began to gradually move to the side streets and all the most beautiful places and building plots were occupied by the newly rich and the church. In the years 1653 to 1720 Hradčany was incorporated inside the new Baroque fortifications surrounding the whole of Prague (remainders of them can be seen in many places) and after the Baroque reconstruction no substantial architectural changes came about.

Present-day Hradčany can be divided into four wholes: Pohořelec, Loretánské Square, Nový Svět and Hradčanské Square.

Today Pohořelec seems like the square of a country town. Its elongated triangular ground-plan, row of small houses adjoining Strahov, houses with arcades, a small church – such is the sight which is often repeated in small Czech towns.

Loretánské Square is a special urban formation. Its base is formed by the long mass of huge Černín Palace (now the Ministry of Foreign Affairs), built perpendicularly to the axis of Hradčany. Deep below it is the Loretto, a place of pilgrimage whose construction was started in 1626. The first part to be built was the chapel called the Santa Casa, a copy of the one which according to a legend was taken by angels from Nazareth to Dalmatia and from there to Italy. And because the Santa Casa could not hold all the believers who pilgrimaged to it its founder Mrs. Benigna Kateřina Lobko-vitz had a roofed gallery built round the chapel so that those who had to remain outside were protected from bad weather. In 1721 the next phase of the building of the Loretto was started with the participation or K. I. Dien-zenhofer. The area in front of the Loretto was laid out and a new façade with a belfry was built under the supervision of this genius. Dienzenhofer had to cope with quite a complicated task, because the huge massif of Černín Palace already stood opposite the Loretto, oppressing everything round it. Moreover, the ground sloped and the façade of the Loretto had to be representative as required by the pomp of a Catholic place of pilgrim-age. Everything turned out well and so Loretanské Square with the Loretto, Černín Palace and the modest area of the Capuchin monastery form a un-ique Baroque complex. Also here in addition to the big place of pilgrimage are the monumental palaces of the powerful and rich nobility, the simple building of the Capuchin monastery and the Church of Our Lady. They form a dramatic and inimitable whole which deserves the attention of every visitor to Hradčany and Prague.

Nový Svět originated in the 15th century. It is a kind of suburb of Hrad-čany, whose character resembles that of the Golden Lane at the Castle. The rising course of this romantic little Hradčany lane, lined with ground-floor or one-storeyed houses, brings a village to mind, especially due to the treetops rising above them from the surrounding gardens. Contrary to the Golden Lane at the Castle the little houses in Nový Svět are still in-habited. The streets called U kasáren, Černínská and Kanovnická connect Nový Svět with Loretanské Square and Hradčanské Square.

The narrow strip between Tuscany Palace and the so-called Little House leads to Hradčanské Square which was once the base and centre of the tributary town of Hradčany. The ancient road from the Castle to the north-west is followed by present Loretánská Street. The historical character of the square has remained undisturbed. Only the glitter and colourfulness of the cars of foreign and home visitors contrast with it.

Úvoz, the road from Pohořelec to the Little Quarter, also belongs to Hradčany. It was once called the Deep Path. It is lined on one side with picturesque groupings of small houses and larger palaces. On the other side there is the depression of Strahov Garden and in the background Petřín Hill. One hundred years ago the wall surrounding Strahov Garden was higher, the garden behind it being woven with many legends about ghosts. The closely placed houses in the middle part of Úvoz, small palaces, walls and arbours bring an Italian environment to mind.

It is possible to walk straight through the streets, squares and courtyards of Hradčany in less than half an hour; strolls through the parallel commu-nications via Úvoz and Nový Svět prolong this period. However, a tour of the accessible Hradčany palaces, church interiors, houses and gardens re-quires several days.

83

78 This place is called **Na Pohořelci** (At Pohořelec). In the foreground are houses built in the 18th century, one of them serving as a toll house. Behind them is the Church of St. Rochus. On the right is the gate of Strahov Monastery.

79 The courtyard of Strahov Monastery is entered from the west through a gate decorated with a statue of the founder of the Premonstratensian order St. Norbert.

80 Standing on the left of the entrance gate of Strahov Monastery is **the Church of St. Rochus** which the Emperor Rudolph II had built for protection against the plague on a cross-shaped ground-plan in a remarkable combination of the Gothic and the Renaissance, perhaps after a design by G. M. Fillippi. The church now serves as the Mussion Exhibition Hall.

81 The Classical façade of the building of Strahov Library is the work of the Czech architect of Italian origin I. Palliardi. The library was built in 1783 and it is considered to be the most outstanding building of the Josephian period. Its sculptured decora-

tion – vases, ornaments and symbolic attributes with a medallion of three Emperor Joseph II – are the work of the sculptor I. Platzer the Younger. Inside this building is the beautiful Philosophical Hall with a rich collection of books.

82 The façade of the abbot's Church of the Assumption of Our Lady was modified in the mid-18th century.

83 The interior of the Strahov abbey church is mainly Baroque. Standing by a wall in the choir is a memorial to the founders of the monastery Prince Vladislav II and the bishop Jindřich Zdík. The side aisle affords access to St. Ursuline's Chapel, where the remains of St. Norbert are housed. W. A. Mozart played the organ of 1746 to 1789 during his sojourn in Prague.

84

85

86

87

84 Situated in a separate building next to the Strahov monastery convent is the **Philosophical Hall,** built from 1782 to 1784. It passes through the two floors of the building and has ceiling frescos by the Viennese court painter A. F. Maulbertsch.

85 The observation terrace above the **Seminary Garden** affords a fine view of Prague from the west especially before evening, when it is lit by the rays of the setting sun.

86 The **Theological Hall,** built from 1671 to 1679, was originally the Strahov monastery library. In the stucco cartouches of the Baroque vault there are wall paintings by a Strahov monk – the painter Siard Nosecky.

87 Aerial view of the **Strahov Premonstratensian Monastery.** It consists of a large group of monastery buildings which are dominated by the Church of the Assumption of Our Lady. It has a trapezoidal groundplan, the total length of its sides exceeding 500 metres. In the course of the years the monastery was reconstructed several times. Its present appearance is Baroque. On the right in the foreground is the abbey building and behind it the building of the chapter and refectory. On the southern side is the summer refectory and in the centre the courtyard and particularly the large Court of Paradise.

88 In 1375 the vice-margrave Aleš of Malkovice founded a community below Strahov which in later years gained the name **Pohořelec** because it was completely burned during the Hussite wars. The photo shows present-day Pohořelec, where is a number of mainly Baroque buildings.

89 The upper corner of Pohořelec ends with Kučera Palace, which has been called the **House at the Golden Ship** (Dům u zlaté lodi) since time immemorial. It is a Rococo plastered building of 1775 to 1780 and was probably designed by the young architect J. J. Wirch. The owner of the house, an imperial officer named Jan Kučera, was a friend of Ludwig van Beethoven.

90 The houses on the northern side of Pohořelec have arcades typical of the squares of medieval towns.

91 **Former St. Elizabeth's Hospital** was founded in 1668 by the abbot of Strahov. Its façade is decorated with a double-branched staircase with a group of statues Pieta, built in 1726.

92 Situated at the place where Loretanská Street meets up with Úvoz is Early Baroque **Trautmansdorf House.**

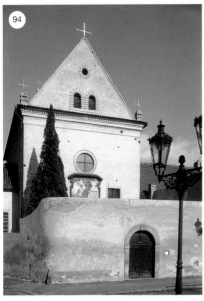

93 **Černín Palace,** now the Ministry of Foreign Affairs of the Czech Republic, was built in the last third of the 17th century by Count Černín of Chudenice. The building work was continued by the grandson of his brother Humprecht Jan Černín of Chudenice. The plans were drafted by the Italian builder P. Caratti, who had settled in Prague, and several prominent architects – G. B. Maderna, D. E. Rossi, G. B. Alliprandi and F. M. Kaňka – participated in realization.

94 Below Černín Palace is the simple **Church of Our Lady** and next to it the Capuchin monastery, the oldest Capuchin monastery in Bohemia. It was built from 1600 to 1602 in the garden of Markéta of Lobkovitz.

95 **View from Petřín** of Úvoz and Loretánské Square. In the foreground Úvoz and in the background on the left the Capuchin Church of Our Lady.

Loretánske Square with the Loretto, Černín Palace and the Capuchin church and monastery form a unique Baroque complex.

96 **The Loretto** is a place of pilgrimage built in the counter-reformation period at the turn of the 17th and 18th centuries. In its steeple there is a carillon which the Little guarter tinsmith Eberhard of Glauchov made in 1694. Its 27 bells were cast by Klaudius Fromm in Amsterdam and the play of bells is the work of the Prague clockmaker Petr Neumann. The Loretto façade facing Loretánské Square is the work of K. I. Dienzenhofer.

97 In the centre of the Loretto is a courtyard with the **Santa Casa,** a copy of the Santa Casa in the Loretto in Italy. The Santa Case, the cottage of the Holy Family, was taken by angels from Nazareth to Dalmatia and from there to Italy according to a legend. At Hradčany in Prague it is the work of G. Orsi.

98 As the Santa Casa could not hold all the believers who pilgrimaged to it the founder of the Loretto Mrs. Benigna Kateřina, wife of Vilém Popel, had a cloister built round it.

99 From 1734 to 1735 **the Church of the Nativity of the Lord** was built on the site of the several times enlarged Loretto chapel under the supervision of J. J. Aichbauer. Its intimate interior captivates the visitor with its unity and purity of style. The fresco The Sacrificing of Christ which decorates it is the work of V. V. Reiner.

100 This folk sandstone sculpture of St. John Nepomuk dates to the late 18th century. It was transferred to the wall in Černínská Street in Nový Svět from South Bohemia, where it was found in the ancient chapel.

101 The small house called **At the Golden Sun** (U zlatého slunce) on the corner of Nový Svět and Černínská Street is a witness of the time when Nový Svět and Černínská Street attracted poets and writers to set the plots of their romantic and mystery stories here. The poor widow in the Hradčany legend about the Loretto bells lived here. It is also here that the story by the novelist J. Arbes about a woman who acquired the beauty of the Muril Madonna was set.

102 On 29 April, the concert master and violin teacher František Ondříček was born in the house called **At the Golden Plough** (U zlatého pluhu). His father Jan Ondříček was a violinist in the popular band of the imperial-royal privileged corps of snipers which performed under the baton of the composer K. Komzák and in which A. Dvořák also played.

103 Outstanding among the tiny houses in romantic Nový Svět is the house called **At the Golden Pear** (U zlaté hrušky) with a well-known restaurant. It is a Baroque building of the first half of the 18th century. It is alleged that in this house, formerly called At Abraham's, there was a bench hewn out of a single piece of stone which came from a church burned by the Hussites. Those who sat on it felt the urge to say at least a short prayer.

104 This graffiti-decorated house on the corner of Kanovnická Street served as an **asylum.** Once standing opposite it was Špitál Gate through which the path leading to the River Brusnice was reached. Adjoining the gate was St. Anthony's Hospital. After 1360 the Hradčany suburb Nový Svět was incorporated in the fortifications of the town. Not until the 17th and 18th centuries was Prague enclosed by new walls. At Hradčany these were built by the castle builder S. Bossi.

105 **The Church of St. John Nepomuk** of 1720 to 1729 was the first church built in Prague by K. I. Dienzenhofer. It was rounded by the Ursuline convent and ranks among Prague's most beautiful Baroque churches. Its interior is particularly charming, due especially to the monumental fresco by V. V. Reiner portraying scenes from the life of St. John Nepomuk. On the high altar and in the side chapels there are paintings by J. K. Liška, brought here from the demolished Church of S. Adalbert.

106 **Kanovnická Street** was called Uršulinská until 1870 because the former Uršuline convent was housed in Talmberg House. It acquired the name Kanovnická because in former times the St. Vitus canons had lived in houses Nos. 66, 67 and 68. In the background in the photo is the rear tract of Martinic Palace.

107 The chapel in the **courtyard of former St. Anthony's Hospital,** founded in 1574, has a Baroque appearance of the late thirties of the 18th century.

108 Standing by the side of Tuscany Palace is **one of the houses of the St. Vitus canons.** It was originally Renaissance, but its present Baroque appearance dates from the latter half of the 18th century. On its façade there is a painting of St. John Nepomuk with Charles Bridge in the background bringing to mind the martyr's death of the saint.

109 Standing in the upper corner of Hradčanské Square is **Martinic Palace** with late Czech Renaissance gables. It was built by an unknown Prague architect on the site of four former Gothic houses, one of which belonged to Charles IV's chronicler, Beneš Krabice of Weitmile. Its later owners included Jaroslav Bořita of Martinic, one of the three persons thrown from a window of Prague Castle at the beginning of the uprising of the Czech Estates in 1618.

110 The counterpart of Prague Castle at the opposite end of Hradčanské Square is **Tuscany Palace.** It was built in the 17th century by the prominent French builder active in Bohemia J. K. Mathey for Count Michal Oskar Thun Honenštejn. It is an Early Baroque building in Roman style with two towers and statues of mythological figures on the attic. Above the door of the balconies are the emblems of the dukes of Tuscany and on the southern corner there is a statue of St. Michael by O. Most.

111 **Loretánská Street.** On the right in the foreground is Hrzán Palace, once the house of the builder of St. Vitus's Cathedral P. Parler. From the late 18th century it was the seat of the

111

chapter deanery. Its present Late Baroque appearance originated in the late 18th century. In its lower façade is a small Gothic window which allegedly belonged to the flat of Prague's executioner. On the left is a cast iron gas candelabrum of the mid-19th century. In the background is St. Benedict's Church attached to the Barnabite convent.

112 The former Hradčany Town Hall is Renaissance and dates in 1588. On its façade there are graffiti with the remainders of the imperial and Hradčany emblems. Set in the Town Hall door is a metal Prague „loket" (59.61 cm) – the official length by means of which cloth was measured in the nearby market-place.

113 The two former **Schwarzenberg Palaces.** It is a valuable work of the Czech Renaissance with an Italian court, rustic graffiti and a lunette cornice.

114 In the past the Museum of Military History was placed in the Schwarzenberg Palace. The photos show this part of its history. The palace as well as the adjoining Salmovský Palace are now owned, by the National Gallery. Placed in the courtyard of the former Museum of Military History in Schwarzenberg Palace were old heavy fire arms.

115 The bronze statue of T. G. Masaryk, the first President of the Czech Republic has been standing at the corner of Salmovský Palace since 2000, as besigned by O. Španiel.

112

113

114

115

116 In the centre of the façade of the Archbishop's Palace is the large emblem of **Archbishop Jan Bedřich of Valdštejn** who took up residence here on 14. 3. 1676. His remains are housed in Valdštejn Chapel in St. Vitus's Cathedral.

117 Hradčanské Square forms the foreground of Prague Castle. With its size and ground-plan it has preserved its medieval appearance even though it is now surrounded on all sides by Renaissance and Baroque palaces. The sloping triangle of this square was once the square of the tributary town of Hradčany. Not until Charles IV fortified and enlarged Hradčany did the original population move to the surrounding streets, freeing the square for the palaces of the clergy and nobility. The southern part of the square afforded access to the Castle by means of a drawbridge spanning the deep ditch of the Royal Castle. In the south-western corner of the square stood the parish Church or St. Benedictine with a monastery and the Town Hall. These buildings have remained in the square, whose present appearance is Baroque. The optical focus of present Hradčanské Square is formed by a Baroque Marian plague column, the work of F. M. Brokoff and one of the few preserved cast iron candelabra with gas lamps of the sixties of the 19th century. In the foreground on the left is the Archbishop's Palace with a Rococo façade decorated with characteristic flat ornaments. Opposite it is Schwarzenberg Palace and in the background Tuscany (Thun-Hohenštejn) Palace.

118 Hradčanské Square with Loretanská Street. After the great fire in the Little Quarter and Hradčany in the mid-16th century Hradčanské Square became a residential enclave in which the nobility built palaces with greenery in the adjoining gardens

116

from the mid-16th to the early 19th century. In the foreground on the right is Schwarzenberg Palace. It was built by Jan of Lobkovitz, later belonging to Petr Vok of Rožmberk and after his death to the Švamberks and finally to the Schwarzenbergs. It represents a Renaissance bastion of aristocratic power and is also an outstanding work of Renaissance architecture. In its neighbourhood is St. Benedictine's Church with the Barnabite convent. The nuns arrived here in 1792, bringing with them the mummified body of the founder of the order Reverend Mother Elekta and placing them in a glass coffin directly in the church. Between the Barnabite convent and Tuscany Palace (only one half of it can be seen in the photo) Loretanská Street runs into Hradčanské Square. On the right, above the greenery of the Seminary Garden, is Strahov Monastery with its dominant formed by the two steeples of the abbey Church of the Assumption of Our Lady.

117

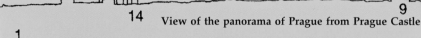

14 View of the panorama of Prague from Prague Castle

9

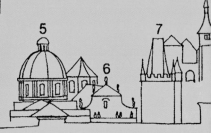

1 Jindřišská Tower
2 Clementinum
3 St Gall's
4 Wilson Station
5 St. John the Baptist's at the Knights of the Cross
6 The Holy Saviour
7 Old Town Bridge Tower
8 St. Giles's
9 Church of the Most Sacred Heart of the Lord
10 Little Quarter Bridge Tower
11 Church of Our Lady of the Snows

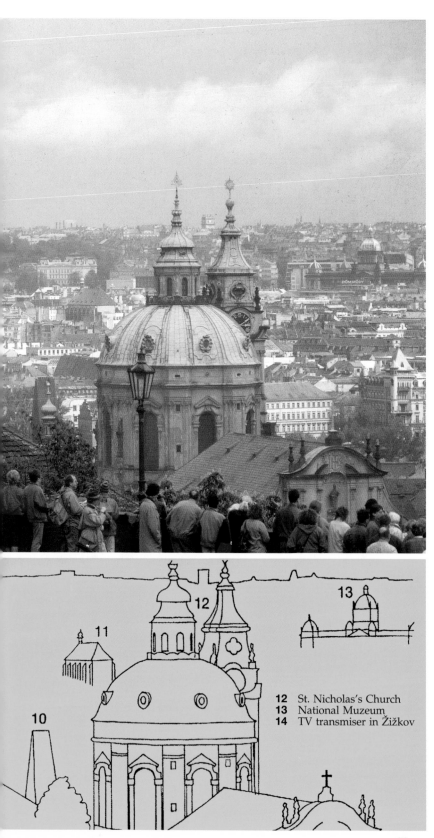

12 St. Nicholas's Church
13 National Muzeum
14 TV transmiser in Žižkov

IV. PRAGUE CASTLE

The magnificent landmark of the historic core of Prague is Prague Castle, which has gazed down on the River Vltava for more than 1100 years. Throughout practically the whole period of its existence it has fulfilled the role of the centre of the Czech state and in this respect it has no rival in Europe as a whole. At first it was the seat of princes and later of Czech kings (on two occasions it even served as the residence of the Roman emperor). In more recent times it was the seat of the offices of the governors, finally becoming the place of work of the presidents of the republic. However, the Castle did not enjoy only the glory and glitter of the ruler's court. Its history has been marked by the almost regular alternation of periods of flourish and building activity with times when it was neglected or heavily damaged by fires and war events.

The oldest period of the Castle is gradually being revealed by archeological research, carried out here unceasingly since 1925. The results of research activity of recent years have shown that the area of the Castle was already settled soon after the mid-9th century. It was not until the last quarter of the 9th century that it became a fortified castle site typical of the early Middle Ages. At that time Bořivoj I, the oldest historically documented prince of the dynasty which derived its origin from legendary Přemysl the Ploughman, transferred his seat here from nearby Levý Hradec. Prague Castle became the central point of the newly built Czech state.

Prague Castle had the best preconditions for the function of a fortified seat of princes. In the south it fell steeply to the River Vltava and on the northern and western sides it was protected by natural gorges. As was usual in those days, the Castle was provided with a fortification system in the form of a rampart, i.e., a huge earthen embankment round its whole periphery. The rampart had an inner structure built from the trunks and branches of oak trees, its outer side being faced with stone masonry. The inner part of the castle site was to a great extent taken up by small frame dwelling-houses. The first stone buildings appeared among them only gradually: the little Church of Our Lady in the western outer bailey at the end of the 9th century, the first at Prague Castle and the second in Bohemia, St. George's Basilica (c. 920), St. Vitus's Rotunda, founded by St. Wenceslas (Václav) only a few years before he was murdered, and the house of the bishop with a chapel in the first half of the 11th century at the latest . Before long a palace of princes was evidently built, but its oldest appearance is unknown. From a description of the ceremonies which took place on the occasion of the installation of Prince Břetislav I on the throne in 1037 (in Cosmas' Chronicle) we know that a stone prince's throne stood on the area of the square náměstí U svatého Jiří of the present. In order that the election of a prince might be valid and recognized, he had to be seated on this throne in front of the eyes of the assembled dignitaries and ordinary people. This explains why there were so many power struggles for the Castle in the 11th and 12th centuries. The rampart did not exist for long on the sloping and rocky ground. From time to time it was necessary to rebuild it. Up to the first half of the 12th century this happened three times on the southern side. One of such thorough reconstructions of the rampart was carried out by Břetislav I after its failure to successfully defend the Castle against Jindřich III (1041). On that occasion it was partly destroyed by fire.

On the feast of St. Wenceslas in 1060 Prince Spytihněv II found that St. Vitus's Rotunda no longer sufficed to hold the crowd of believers. He therefore had it demolished and founded a much more spacious basilica consecrated to SS. Wenceslas and Adalbert on its site. The southern apse of the former rotunda was preserved along with the grave of the principal provincial patron saint and formed a part of the new building. Spytihněv II died in the following year and the construction work was continued by his brother Vratislav II. His constant disputes with his brother, Bishop Jaromír, after 1068 forced Prince Vratislav II to move his seat to Vyšehrad. This undoubtedly slowed down building activity at the Castle: St. Vitus's Basilica, which was damaged by fire in 1091, was wholly completed as late as 1096. It was Prince Soběslav I that finally transferred the seat of princes back to Prague Castle towards the end of his reign. The thorough reconstruction which he began in 1135 transformed the Přemyslid castle site into a real medieval castle. With the exception of the western outer bailey the

120   The Third Courtyard with the Old Deanery and the cathedral.

whole periphery was surrounded by a huge wall faced with cretaceous marly limestone. Its southern side was reinforced with solid turrets of various shapes. The palace of princes, later the royal palace, was built at the same time as the wall. The architect concerned located it on a slope on the southern side so that its outer wall also formed a part of the fortification line.

The entrance to the Castle was guarded by huge prismatic towers: in the west the White Tower (now standing in the western wing between the Second and Third Courtyards), a nameless tower on the southern side (now inserted in the Old Royal Palace) and the Black Tower in the east. The wall was so well-built that it fulfilled the function of the main fortification element up to the end of the Middle Ages. Parts of it can still be seen in many places at the Castle.

During its siege by Konrád Znojemský (in 1142) the Castle defended itself, but it was damaged by a great fire. St. George's Basilica and the bishop's house had to be thoroughly rebuilt. The date of the completion of the Romanesque reconstruction is generally considered to be the year 1185, when the palace chapel was consecrated to All Saints.

The Romanesque reconstruction of Prague Castle was so thorough that during the remainder of the 12th and throughout the 13th century no basic changes were necessary. The „monastery of the church of Prague" originated to the north of the Basilica of SS. Vitus, Wenceslas and Adalbert (the seat of the St. Vitus chapter) and a single-naved church consecrated to St. Bartholomew and the first masonry-built houses sprang up on the area of the Third Courtyard. Buildings also came into being in the square U svatého Jiří. Přemysl Otakar II had the royal palace reconstructed and enlarged and the fortifications strengthened with new ditches. After his death in 1280 a part of the fortification wall, St. George's Convent and the seat of the chapter collapsed into the gorge of the little River Brusnice after heavy rains. A fire in 1303 caused damage to the Royal Palace and the building was evidently not repaired in the following years.

When Prince Charles, later King Charles IV, returned to Prague from France in 1333 he found the royal seat in a very neglected state. „Prague Castle was so desolate, demolished and broken that it collapsed to the ground from the times of King Otakar II. On this site we have had a new and beautiful palace built at great cost, as the passer-by can now see", wrote the Emperor in his autobiography Vita Caroli. While he resided in the burgrave's house he had the reconstruction of the Royal Palace started soon after his return.

Thanks to his efforts the Prague bishopric was raised to an archbishopric in 1344 and in the same year King John of Luxembourg founded a new cathedral, consecrated to St. Vitus. Its first builder, Matthias of Arras, began the construction work from the east end. Until his death (in 1352) he sufficed to build a part of the ring of choir chapels and the pillars for the vault of the high choir. His work was continued of the talented architect Peter Parler, who arrived in Prague at the age of twenty-three. He completed and vaulted the high choir with a gallery and chapels, St. Wenceslas's Chapel and the Golden Portal. He also founded the transverse nave and started the construction of the great steeple.

After his father's death building activity was continued by Václav IV. The period of his reign was marked in particular by Parler's new building of All Saints Church, which replaced the older palace chapel. Václav Hájek of Libočany referred to it (in a report about the destructive fire of 1541) as a building „which as a beautiful and costly work was built at great expense by Charles IV and decorated with stone carvings and other stone-cutter's work and beautified with magnificent glasses". In the late 15th century the Royal Palace was rebuilt and enlarged by the addition of two transverse wings (the present Diet wing, which was narrower at that time, on the northern side and the narrow southern wing). In the period devoted to this reconstruction the ruler may have taken up residence at the Royal Court in the Old Town (Staré Město). Building activity at the Castle, which then clearly continued with less intensity, was definitely interrupted by the king's death and the outbreak of the Hussite wars in 1419. For the Castle the war period meant only disasters: right at its very beginning it was looted by the people of Prague and later occupied by the garrison of the Emperor Sigismund. He hurriedly had himself crowned as the king of Bohemia, whereupon he immediately left the Castle, taking the coronation jewels with him.

Prague Castle remained deserted even after the termination of the Hussite wars. True, it continued to be the official royal seat where important state events took place, but it was the Royal Court that was the real residence of the sovereign. A change came about as late as during the reign of Vladislav Jagiello, who began to consider returning to the Castle. After the periods of unrest in 1483 he did not feel safe in the town and before long realized his intention. However, the Castle urgently needed to be reconstructed, its fortification system in particular being obsolete. Benedikt Ried was summoned to carry out the work. The improved fire arms, easily capable of overshooting the gorge of the River Brusnice, represented the greatest danger. For this reason a parkan wall strengthened with three cannon towers (from the east these are Daliborka, the White Tower and the Powder Tower – Mihulka) were built on the northern side. The older parkan wall on the southern side was strengthened with three cannon bastions and the eastern gate was provided with a fortified gate in front of it. Buildings and interiors intended to meet the purposes of royal representation originated. The most outstanding of them is the Vladislav Hall, built on the site of an older big hall of the time of Charles IV. B. Ried kept only the peripheral wall and provided the enormous hall with a curved vault with five fields and no inner supports, thus creating the biggest secular vaulted interior in Europe of that time.

Although Vladislav became the king of Hungary in 1490 and moved to Buda, he took care to ensure that the reconstruction of Prague Castle was completed „for the virtue of us and the crown, for the pleasure and grace of future kings and for the honour of this kingdom" as he himself expressed. The first manifestations of the new style, the Renaissance, also reached Prague via the Italian artists working on Buda Castle. The big windows of the Vladislav Hall and especially the capitals of its pilasters and half-columns are the oldest Renaissance details in Bohemia. B. Ried enlarged the Royal Palace still further by adding the Louis Wing, built from 1502 to 1510. The attempt of Vladislav Jagiello to ensure the completion of St. Vitus's Cathedral ended merely with the foundation for the northern tower.

After the death of the young Ludvík Jagiello in 1526 the period of reign of the Jagiello dynasty came to an end and the throne was succeeded to by Ludvík's brother-in-law Ferdinand Hapsburg. He kept his promise at least in the first period of his reign and resided permanently in Prague. Later he was represented by a governer – Archduke Ferdinand of Tyrol. Ferdinand's most important deed as regards the appearance of the Castle was the founding of the Royal Garden (Královská zahrada) on the site of older vineyards in the northern outer bailey. So as to make it easily accessible it was necessary to build a bridge across the gorge of the River Brusnice and as a result the Castle gained a northern gate. The bridge itself was built of wood and it was borne by five huge stone piers. In 1538 the construction of a summer palace, a beautiful building which had the appearance of having been transferred directly from Renaissance Italy, was commenced in the Royal Garden with the participation of Italian artists. In 1541 a fire broke out in the Little Quarter which spread rapidly and in a short space of time affected not only the Little Quarter, but also the whole Castle and the small town of Hradčany. Several years elapsed before the extensive damage was repaired. The same fire also resulted in a change of the appearance of the Castle, since it freed space for the new construction of big, imposing Renaissance Pernštejn and Rožmberk Palaces.

Prague Castle was enriched with a number of buildings by the architect Bonifáz Wolmut, who fulfilled the function of the royal architect from 1556. In particular he gradually built the upper floor and roof of the Royal Summer Palace, the characteristic helmet of the great steeple of St. Vitus's Cathedral, the new vault of the Diet and the tribune of the supreme scribe in this interior, and the big Ball-games Hall. The private residential quarters of the sovereign began to be transferred from the Royal Palace (where important offices were concentrated to an ever greater extent) to the southern wing already during the reign of Ferdinand I. Its construction (at the place of contact of the southern and the central wing) was continued particularly by Rudolph II, who resided permanently at Prague Castle from 1583. Thus for the second time in the course of its existence the Castle served as the residence of the Emperor and the centre of the empire as a whole. Rudolph won renown as a passionate collector, but he was also an enthusiastic builder. He laid the foundation of the present central wing by building a narrow wing on the outer side of the western Romanesque wall. The ground-floor was occupied by stables, while collections (an art chamber and a picture gallery) were installed on the upper floors. The Emperor newly founded the northern wing in which he had two big halls built above spacious stables. These halls (the present Spanish Hall and the Rudolph Gallery) were also intended to house collections. However, Rudolph also continued in the erection of buildings in the Royal Garden and in the northern outer bailey behind Stag Ditch (named after the enclosure for deer, which was established here during his reign). The so-called Lions' Court, a summer riding-school, a pheasantry, an aviary, a pond, a shooting-ground and other structures were gradually built.

121 Rudolph II. A bust from the old collections of Prague Castle.

Only two buildings can be attributed to the short reign of the Emperor Matthias, namely the Matthias Gate (the main western entrance) and a small round pavilion in the southern gardens. The seat of the Emperor was again – and this time definitely – transferred to Vienna.

In 1618 two Catholic governors and their secretary were thrown from a window of the Czech Office. This defenstration ignited the uprising of the Czech Estates and the Thirty Years War, which affected the greater part of Europe. Prague Castle was occupied twice without any resistance, first by a Saxon and then by a Swedish army. Its losses were great especially during the Swedish attack, when a large part of Rudolph's collections was stolen. Building activity continued at the Castle also during the unfavourable war period, however. It was necessary to repair the sustained damage and, moreover, interiors were built for the empress in the southern wing and for her entourage in the central one.

In the first half of the 18th century Prague Castle first of all witnessed the solemn coronation of Charles VI as the Czech king (1723). The sanctification of John Nepomuk six years later was also of a solemn character. Building activity was recommenced at the Castle as late as the reign of the Empress Maria Theresa. The beginning of her period of rule was marked by war events. Firstly, in 1741, Prague was occupied by French and Saxon troops and in 1744 by a Prussian army. The Empress had former Rožmberk Palace rebuilt and converted into the Institute for Gentlewomen, laying the foundation stone for this reconstruction in 1754. Just one year later the last extensive reconstruction of the Castle was carried out, the result of which was the unification of all the wings of the so-called New Palace. The projects for both these wide-scale building activities were drawn up by the court architect Nicola Pacassi.

Even after the completion of the reconstruction, which lent the prevailingly medieval castle the character of a chateau seat, the Castle was not used by the imperial court. On the contrary, during the reign of Joseph II a number of buildings (the Riding-school, St. George's Convent, the Ballgames Hall and the Royal Summer Palace) was placed at the disposal of the army. The royal seat was not adequately maintained in the 19th century either. Certain modifications realized for Ferdinand I, who after his abdication in 1848 resided here with a small court, and before the planned, but never realized coronation of Franz Joseph I. Otherwise the Castle rather fell into a state of desolation.

It was finally the Union for the Completion of St. Vitus's Cathedral that began building activity of a greater extent when in 1859 it had the medieval torso of the cathedral repaired. From 1873 the building process proceeded after a plan by Josef Mocker and later by Kamil Hilbert until the cathedral gained its present appearance. The construction work was successfully completed for the celebrations of the millennium of St. Wenceslas in 1929. The Union entrusted the decoration of the cathedral to a whole number of young Czech artists.

When the independent Czechoslovak Republic originated in 1918 Prague Castle fully regained its function of the seat of the head of State. However, after years of neglect the buildings intended for the purposes of State representation needed a number of repairs. From 1920 these were the concern of the architect Josip Plečnik, a professor at the Academy of Applied Art in Prague. The first thing he did was to newly lay out the southern gardens and supplement them with a number of small and larger structures. He designed the modifications of the First Courtyard and the adjoining interiors of the western wing and also drew up a project concerning the level of the Third Courtyard, its paving and monolith and the so-called Bulls' Staircase. For President T. G. Masaryk the first architect of Prague Castle designed a study and other interiors of his quarters intended for representative purposes on the second floor of the southern and central wings. After his departure in 1936 the repair work was continued by Otto Rothmayer and Pavel Janák. This was after World War II, which brought a halt to all building activity at the Castle.

The building activities acquired a reconstruction character to an ever greater extent, the historic buildings regaining their original appearance. In 1958 Prague Castle was declared National Cultural Monument No. 1. This certainly contributed to the fact that great attention was devoted to its maintenance even in the period in which inadequate care was taken of other historic monuments.

A whole number of reconstructions was realized from the Fifties, but this time, with a different approach to monuments. Most of them fulfilled their purpose, i.e., the preservation of valuable buildings for the future. Fortunately, some too radical or prevailingly politically motivated proposals were not realized. Wide-scale reconstructions and the unceasing maintenance of monuments along with restoration work meant endless systematic and consistent work at Prague Castle. Many places and buildings are still awaiting attention in order to be made accessible to the public.

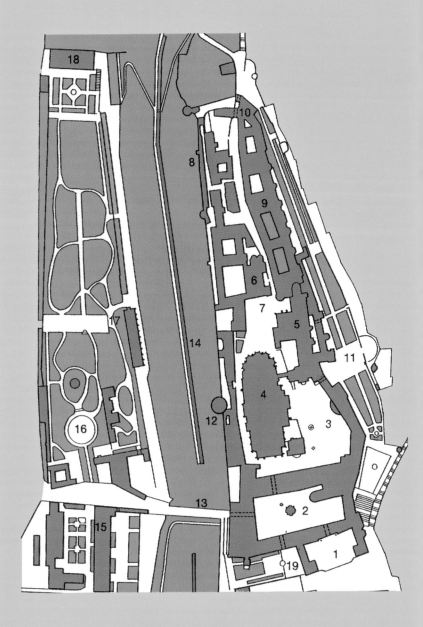

Plan of Prague Castle

1 First Courtyard
2 Second Courtyard
3 Third Courtyard
4 St. Vitus' Cathedral
5 Old Royal Palace
6 St. George's Basilica
7 Náměstí U sv. Jiří
8 Zlatá ulička
9 Institute of Gentlewomen
10 Lobkovitz Palace

11 Garden „Na valech"
12 Mihulka
13 Prašný most
14 Stag Ditch
15 Riding-school
16 Royal Garden
17 Ball-games Hall
18 Royal Summer Palace
19 Fourth Courtyard and Garden
   „Na Baště"

125 **The western entrance** has been the main entrance ever since the beginnings of Prague Castle. Its present appearance was determined by a radical reconstruction carried out during the reign of the Empress Maria Theresa. Then the last of the ditches of the western fortifications was filled-in and the First Courtyard with the function of a cour d'honneur was built.

126 **Maria Theresa and Joseph II** are brought to mind by their monograms on the pedestals of the grille gates.

127 Forming a part of the **western wing** is the manneristic Matthias Gate (Matyášova brána), considered to be the first Baroque secular structure in Prague (1614).

128 **The Staircase of Honour** leads to the reception salons on the first floor of the southern wing. It was built by Nicola Pacassi, the chief architect of the Theresian reconstruction, and the sculptor Ignác František Platzer. It is now used as the entrance for state visitors.

129 **The passage in the western wing** leads to the Second Courtyard, which also originated as the result of the filling-in of the ditch, this time already in the 16th century.

130 The interior of **the Chapel of the Holy Rood** mostly features the Neo-Baroque style dating from the mid–19th century. The ceiling is decorated with painted scenes from the Old Testament.

131 **The dominant of the Second Courtyard** is a Romanesque sandstone fountain, named Kohl's Fountain after the creator of its sculptured decoration.

132 Its time of origin falls in the period of reign of Leopold I, a fact documented by a cartouche with his monogram on the parapet.

133 The foundation of the Central Wing separating the Second and Third Courtyards is a Romanesque wall dating after 1135. This huge wall, whose front side is built of cretaceous marly limestone ashlars, formed the main defence line of the Castle throughout the Middle Ages.

134 One of the most valuable of the paintings preserved in the Picture Gallery of Prague Castle is The Flagellation of Christ by Jacop Robusti, called Tintoretto (oil on canvas, after the mid–16th century). The work was purchased for the Castle collections in 1648 by Archduke Leopold Vilém, who built-up a new picture gallery after the carrying away of the Rudolphian collections.

135 Petrus Paulus Rubens's painting Assembly of the Olympian Gods (oil on canvas, c. 1602). The biggest canvas in the Picture Gallery of Prague Castle portrays the conflict between the goddess Juno (embodiment of the home order and matrimonial faithfulness) and Venus, the goddess of love and beauty. It is not known how the painting found its way into the collections of the Castle.

136 The present Picture Gallery can now be only a remote reminder of the enormous wealth of fine works of art, scientific apparatuses and technical gadgets, and products of nature and curiosities in which Prague Castle abounded during the reign of Rudolph II. The most beautiful interior of the Picture Gallery of Prague Castle is the former stable, built in Rudolph II's reign. It has a remarkable vault with plastic coffers and several original stone jambs.

137 The smaller painting of Diana and Her Entourage by an unknown Netherlandish painter of the 17th century is painted on copper plate.

141

138 Plečnik's Hall of Columns, named after its creator, originated in the years 1927 to 1931 as a part of the modifications of Prague Castle for the Czech president T. G. Masaryk. This monumental interior was created by the removal of all the original floors. The use of galleries with columns of perfectly worked granite bear witness to the fact that Plečnik was inspired by antique architecture. The forwardly situated staircase was built-in additionally in the course of the modifications carried out in 1975.

139 Some other modifications were carried out in Plečnik's spirit by his pupil and co-worker architect Otto Rothmayer. The present forms of the **Wedge Passage and the Rothmayer Hall** are his work.

140 The biggest interior of the reception salons is **the Spanish Hall** (width 21m, length 43 m, height 12 m), built originally for the collections of Rudolph II in the early 17th century. Only a part of the stucco reliefs on the two longer walls has been preserved. The greater part of the decoration of the hall originated from 1866 to 1868, when it was modified for the coronation of Franz Joseph I as the Czech king.

141 The **Hapsburg Salon** with a portrait gallery of Maria Theresa's family has preserved its original appearance. The three big portraits with whole figures on the right represent the Empress, her consort Francis Stephen of Lothringia and his son Joseph II.

142 Hanging in the Throne Room is a painting by the Austrian painter L. Bucher which faithfully portrays the coronation of Ferdinand V in St. Vitus' Cathedral in 1836.

143 The **Brožík Salon** is wholly dominated by an oil painting The Message of King Ladislav Pohrobek to the French Court in 1457. It was painted in Paris in 1878.

142

143

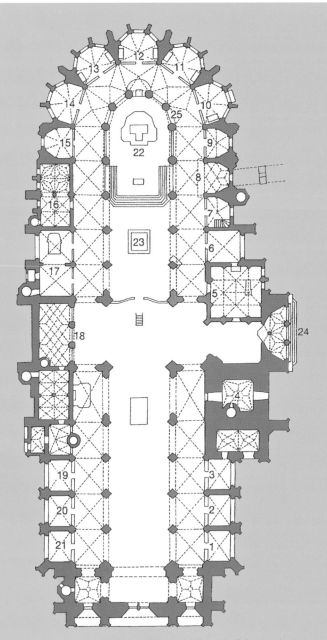

Ground-plan of St. Vitus' Cathedral

1 St. Ludmilla's Chapel
2 Chapel of the Tomb of God
3 Thun Chapel
4 Great Tower (Hazmburk Chapel)
5 St. Wenceslas' Chapel
6 Martinic Chapel
7 Chapel of the Holy Rood (entrance to the royal tomb)
8 Royal Oratory
9 Valdštejn Chapel
10 Chapel of St. John Nepomuk
11 Saxon Chapel
12 Chapel of Our Lady
13 Chapel of St. John the Baptist
14 Old Archbishop's Chapel
15 St. Anne's Chapel
16 Old Sacristy
17 St. Sigismund's Chapel
18 Wolmut's choir (choir chapel)
19 New Archbishop's Chapel
20 Swarzenberg Chapel
21 Chapel of St. Agnes Česká
22 High altar
23 Royal (Colin's) Mausoleum
24 Golden Portal
25 Tomb of St. John Nepomuk

144

145 All three western portals of the cathedral are provided with bronze doors with reliefs (V. H. Brunner together with O. Spaniel, 1927–1929). The decoration of the middle, double entrance brings important scenes from the history of the building to mind. The detail in the photograph pertains to the construction of the Gothic cathedral. The lower relief depicts Matthias of Arras. Behind him two men can be seen carrying a finished hewn ashlar to the places it is to occupy. Wholly in the background can be seen the demolished Basilica of St. Vitus, St. Wenceslas and St. Adalbert of the 11th century.

146 View from the west across the new part of the cathedral of the choir with the high altar.

147 A valuable panel altar, a North Italian work of the 14th century, decorates St. Agnes's Chapel (the Barton family of Dobenín).

148 The so-called Čimelice Ark with a scene The Worship of the Three Kings from the early 16th century is situated in the Schwarzenberg Chapel.

149 The capitals of the pillars were hewn by stonemasons in the 19th and 20th centuries with the same care as in the Middle Ages. Their decoration is, however, much richer.

150 The so-called Bílek's Altar on the wall of the New Sacristy in the northern side aisle (relief The Crucified of 1899; the altar as a whole dates in 1927).

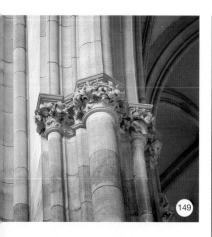

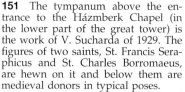

151 The tympanum above the entrance to the Házmberk Chapel (in the lower part of the great tower) is the work of V. Sucharda of 1929. The figures of two saints, St. Francis Seraphicus and St. Charles Borromaeus, are hewn on it and below them are medieval donors in typical poses.

152 The mosaic The Baptism of Christ was designed by M. Švabinský for St. Ludmila's Chapel. It was realized in 1953.

153 Detail of the door of the Choir Chapel below Wolmut's music choir. The figures of St. Wenceslas and St. Vitus rank in the series of reliefs of Czech patron saints.

154 View of the transverse nave, which forms a partition between the old and the new part of the cathedral from the level of the inner triforium. In the year 1924 Wolmut's music choir, transferred from its original place, was built-in into the northern arm. The big organ with Rococo decoration dates in 1763, but it is no longer functional.

155 The big emblem of the Czechoslovak Republic, executed with the use of the mosaic technique on the wall of the southern arm of the transverse nave. On the central shield there is the emblem of Bohemia. The basic shield has five fields: in the upper row Slovakia and Sub- Carpathian Russia, in the middle one Moravia and Silesia and in the lower one the Těšín, Opava and Racibórz regions.

156 The ordinary visitor does not see the interesting vault of the **Choir Chapel.** Apart from the real net ribbed vault there is another net of stone ribs situated loosely in the space below the vault. On the pillars of the intersecting point of the main and the transverse nave there are gilded statues of Czech patron saints. These wooden Baroque sculptures originally stood on the pillars of the choir.

157 **The Old Sacristy** also has an interesting vault above its two-part interior. True, the two halves differ as regards their vaulting and the density and profiling of the ribs. However, they have common use for the hanging coping stone. The two vaults were built by Peter Parler, but he had to adapt his ideas to the work started by his predecessor in the eastern half (in the photograph).

158 Inserted in the pointed window in the **western façade** is a rosette of a diameter of 10.6 m. When viewed from outside the beauty of the stone tracery stands out. The fillings of coloured glass are visible only on the inside. The individual phases of The Creation of the World (realized from 1926 to 1928 after a design by F. Kysela) are symbolically expressed in the individual parts.

159 The large composition with the theme **The Holiest Trinity** after a cartoon by M. Švabinský covers the area of the three windows in the east end of the high choir. The detailed photograph shows the figures of Our Lady and St. Ludmilla from the left-hand side window. Kneeling below them is Prince Spytihněv II, who founded the Basilica of St. Vitus in 1060.

160 The biggest of all the church windows fills the southern façade of the transverse nave. M. Švabinský designed a portrayal of **The Last Judgement for it** (the design dates in 1937 and its realization in 1939).

161 The upper part of the window in St. Luamilla's Chapel. The decoration of the window and the walls of this chapel were designed by M. Švabinský. The glazing of the window with the theme of The Sending Down of the Holy Spirit glows with beautiful, rich colours.

162 The lower parts of the windows of the high choir with important figures from Czech history are in the interior of the inner triforium and are in fact visible only from here.

163 Great attention on the part of visitors is enjoyed by the window of **the New Archbishop's Chapel,** created after a design by A. Mucha in 1931. Smaller scenes from the life of SS. Cyril and Method are grouped round the central field (the bigger section of the photograph on the left).

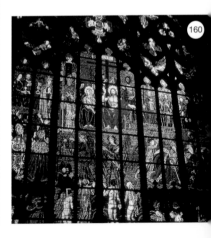

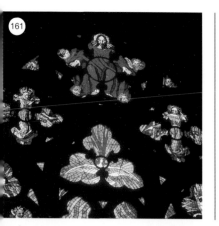

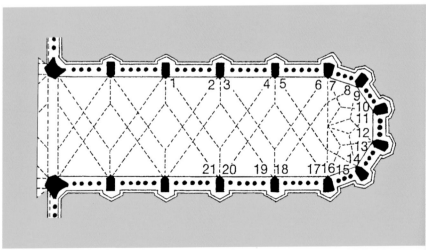

Portrait Gallery of the Inner Triforium (Medieval Part)

1 Václav of Radeč, master builder
2 Matthias of Arras, architect
3 Petr Parler, architect
4 Ondřej Kotík, master builder
5 Beneš Krabice of Weitmile, master builder
6 Václav of Luxembourg
7 Jan Jindřich, Margrave of Moravia, brother of Charles IV
8 Queen Blanche of Valois
9 Queen Anne of the Palatinate
10 Empress Anna Svidnická
11 Empress Eliška of Pomerania
12 Emperor Charles IV
13 King John of Luxembourg
14 Queen Eliška Přemyslovna
15 King Václav IV, son of Charles IV
16 Queen Johanna of Bavaria
17 Arnošt of Pardubice, arcibishop
18 Jan Očko of Vlašim, arcibishop
19 Jan of Jenštejn, arcibishop
20 Mikuláš Holubec, master builder
21 Bušek Leonardův, master bulder

164 From the gallery of the inner triforium the Emperor and king **Charles IV** still gazes down on the finished work. Along with a bust of Eliška of Pomerania, his fourth consort, his bust is set in the axial field and portraits of other members of the royal family are concentrated nearby in the eastern part.

165 The directors of the building work and the two architects are portrayed in sculptures in the triforium. The photograph shows us the bust of **Matthias of Arras.**

166 The portrait of the second architect of the cathedral, **Peter Parler,** may be a self-portrait.

167 In the new part of the cathedral the triforium continues with busts of persons who completed the building of the cathedral. A portrait of **Josef Mocker** occupies a place of honour on the southern side.

168 The sculptured portrait of the architect **Kamil Hilbert,** who successfully completed the building of the cathedral in 1929.

169 This view was once reserved solely for the sovereign and his nearest ones. The shot of the **Royal Oratory** shows the white marble mausoleum in the centre of the choir. It was produced by the Netherlandish sculptor A. Colin for Ferdinand I, his consort Anne Jagiello and their son Maximilian II. The work originated in his workshop in Innsbruck. The individual parts were transported to Prague and definitely put together in 1589. The ornamental Renaissance grille is the work of the Prague locksmith J. Schmidthammer. Concealed below ground level, under Colin's mausoleum, is the royal tomb in which the remains of the Czech kings and other members of the ruling families lie at rest.

170 The windows of the old part of the cathedral mostly come from the last quarter of the 19th century. Their original glazing has not been preserved. The photograph shows the window of **the Martinic Chapel** with the figures of saints after a design by J. Mocker and F. Sequens.

171 The altar in **St. Sigismund's Chapel** ranks among the few examples of Baroque furnishings preserved in the cathedral after its re-Gothization. It comes from the Thirties of the 18th century and has a conspicuous surface finish in red, gold and silver.

172 The epitaph of **Count Leopold Šlik,** who was the supreme chancellor, originated in 1723. Outstanding Baroque artists (H. E. Fischer or Erlach, F. M. Kaňka, M. B. Braun) participated in its realization.

173

174

175

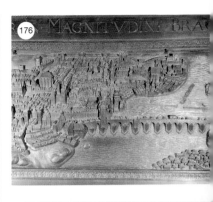

176

177

173 **The portal of the Old Sacristy** with blind tracery in the tympanum. Behind the door of the 19th century there is another original medieval door wing. On the rich leaf console next to the entrance is a statue of the Archangel Michael (17th century).

174 The memorial to the archbishop of Prague **Cardinal Bedřich Schwarzenberg** is the work of J. V. Myslbek of the years 1891 to 1895. The monumental statue is situated on the choir gallery on the northern side.

175 In the axis of the choir behind the high altar there is a tomb of 1840 below which the **remains** of the chief patron saint of the cathedral, **St. Vitus,** lie at rest. The architecture was designed by J. Kranner and the statue of St. Vitus was created by E. Max.

176 Hanging between the pillars of the choir gallery are large oak panels with a relief portrayal of events which took place in Prague at the beginning of the Thirty Years War. The detail in the photograph is a part of the relief **The Flight of Fridrich of the Palati-**

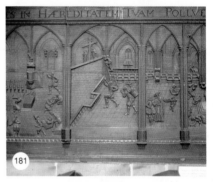

nate from Prague after the Battle on the White Mountain.

177 The masterly works which originated in the Parler workshop include the console with Adam and Eve, intended for the statue of Christ behind the high altar.

178 Some wall paintings of the 14th century have been preserved to the present. The photograph portrays **The Worship of the Three Kings** in the Chapel of the Holy Relics (Saxon).

179 The tombs of the Přemyslid princes and kings in the choir chapels came from the Parler workshop. According to preserved bills we know that at least the figure of Přemysl Otakar I was hewn by Peter Parler himself.

180 The large tomb of St. John Nepomuk was realized after a design by J. E. Fischer of Erlach in silver from 1733 to 1736. The saint is kneeling on the sarcophagus, raised by angels. The balustrade of variously coloured marble with silver sculptures, a red baldachin and freely hanging figures of flying angels are somewhat later supplements of the tomb.

181 Another of the reliefs recalls the plundering of the cathedral by the Calvinists in 1619.

182 The Royal Oratory, built for Vladislav Jagiello, evidently replaced a similar interior of the time of Charles IV. Instead of ribs its vault has dry

branches which also spread into the vault proper. The balustrade with the provincial emblems, seemingly hanging freely, is also created of woven branches.

183 **It is the eastern wall of St. Wenceslas' Chapel** that has the most important place in the programme of decoration of this central interior, which forms a kind of „cathedral in a cathedral". Standing above the altar with a Gothic painting The Crucifixion there is a statue of St. Wenceslas on a profiled cornice. It is one of the most beautiful works of Czech sculpture of the Luxembourg period. The figure of the saints hewn from cretaceous marly limestone and the polychrome are of modern origin. Linking up with the statue is a wall painting of about 1509: two angels on the sides and other provincial patrons, St. Sigismund and St. Vitus (on the left), St. Adalbert and St. Ludmilla (on the right). Higher up, on the sides of the window, there are portraits of King Vladislav Jagiello, during whose reign the wall paintings on the upper part of the walls of the chapel were executed, and his third consort Anne de Foix-

Candale. The upper part of the restored tomb of St. Wenceslas can be seen in the foreground.

184 Kneeling Charles IV as a donor from the scene depicting The Crucifixion. The gilded relief background is a typical element of the decoration of the walls.

185 The murder of St. Wenceslas at Stará Boleslav is brought to mind in the chapel by a fine painting by the monogramist IW. It is dated in 1543 and hangs on a pillar near the northern portal.

186 The lower part of the decoration of the walls of the chapel originated at the time of Charles IV. Individual scenes of the Passion cycle are painted below the cornice. The space between them is filled with polished precious stones. The gaps between the stones are gilded.

187 From St. Wenceslas's Chapel access can be gained by means of a mounted door with seven locks to the **Crown Chamber,** where the coronation jewels of the Czech kings are kept. The oldest of the set as a whole is the crown, made in 1346. It is decorated with pearls and precious stones. The sceptre and the orb represent Renaissance artistic craft work of the first half of the 16th century and did not originally belong to the Czech crown, called St. Wenceslas's crown.

188   St. Vitus' Cathedral can be seen from the large Third Courtyard only from an adequate distance. This explains why its southern façade with the main steeple seems so monumental. It was reckoned already at Charles' time that this façade would be the main one. The ceremonial triple-axis entrance, the so-called Golden Portal (Zlatá brána), was also built here. This name was certainly derived from the gold colour of the background of the mosaic The Last Judgement, which was set in place here in 1371. Above the Golden Portal there is a large pointed window in the southern front transverse nave.

189   The interior of the Golden Portal had to be reconstructed to a considerable extent. The consoles and canopies for the statues were newly hewn after the preserved remainders. The

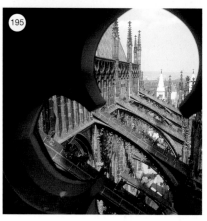

decoration of the modern mosaic The Crucifixion is the work of K. Svolinský.

190 Detail of the bronze relief of the month of September from the grille which closes the Golden Portal (it was designed by J. Hořejc and realized in 1955).

191 This bronze statue of St. George (a precise casting of the original of 1373) stands in the Third Castle Courtyard on a socle realized after a design by J. Plečnik. The exit wall of the Old Deanery indicates the Romanesque origin of the building, which was originally the seat of Prague's bishops. The low ground-floor building which adjoins this façade protects the foundations of the chapel.

192 Sigismund, the biggest bell of St. Vitus's Cathedral, was cast by T. Jaroš in 1549. It hangs on the first floor of the great steeple (behind the window with a gold grille) and weighs 18 tons. It is the third bell bearing this name and of this size. The two previous ones were destroyed.

193 The gallery of the great steeple offers an unusual view not only of the Castle, but also of the Little Quarter (Malá Strana) and other parts of the city. In the foreground a part of the Third Courtyard with granite paving after a design by Josip Plečnik and a part of the façade or the southern wing with a balcony.

194 The bust of St. Vitus from the upper (outer) triforium of the cathedral. Busts of Jesus Christ, the Virgin Mary and all the then patron saints of the Czech kingdom are hewn on the pillars of the eastern part of the choir.

195 The supporting system of the choir part of the cathedral is a remarkable work of Peter Parler's workshop.

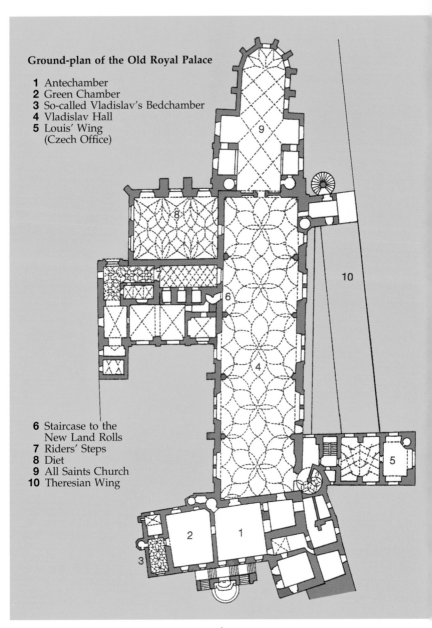

Ground-plan of the Old Royal Palace

1 Antechamber
2 Green Chamber
3 So-called Vladislav's Bedchamber
4 Vladislav Hall
5 Louis' Wing
  (Czech Office)

6 Staircase to the
  New Land Rolls
7 Riders' Steps
8 Diet
9 All Saints Church
10 Theresian Wing

196 Detail of the carved joist of the **Bulls' Staircase,** which connects the Third Courtyard with the Garden on the Ramparts (Zahrada Na valech) (after a design by J. Plečnik).
197 The Eagle Fountain in front of the entrance to the Old Royal Palace indicates the older ground level in this part of the Third Courtyard.
198 The rich Late Gothic vault of so-called **Vladislav's Bedchamber** makes it possible to imagine the magnificence and the colourfulness of medieval interiors. This interior served the representation purposes of Vladislav Jagiello and on the vault there are the em-

blems of the countries over which he reigned (before 1490).
199 The one-time **ground-floor of the Romanesque palace** (after 1135) covers a large area and still has its original barrel vault.
200 The easternmost of the interiors of the Gothic floor of the Old Royal Palace has no floor in order that the ascertained remainders of the living rooms from the Romanesque period may be seen. In the background the western wall of All Saints Chapel of the 12th century with two portals situated one above the other (the upper one led to the tribune of princes).

201 The **Vladislav Hall** is the biggest and the most effective interior of the Old Royal Palace. It was built from 1493 to 1500 by B. Ried and mainly served the purposes of royal representation.

202 The crowned L brings to mind King Louis Jagiello, after whom the **Louis' Wing** (Ludvíkovo křídlo) is named. The Early Renaissance portal connected the two rooms of the Czech Office.

203 Two governors along with their secretary were thrown from this window on 23 May, 1618. In spite of the considerable height above ground of the window all three survived their fall. The event ignited the unsuccessful anti-Hapsburg uprising of the Estates, which meant the beginning of the Thirty Years War.

204 The **Office of the Imperial Court Council** is still furnished with 17th-century furniture.

205 **Paintings of Czech kings** from the Hapsburg dynasty decorate the walls of the Office of the Imperial Court Council.

206 The richly decorated **portal of the Vladislav Hall** on the choir of All Saints Church terminates with the emblem of the Czech kingdom.

207 The Church of All Saints was built by Peter Parler on the site of a Romanesque chapel. Its magnificent building was unfortunately destroyed by fire in 1541 and it was not until forty years later that it was renewed. True, at that time the church was enlarged, but it acquired a far simpler appearance with a lower vault and smaller windows. It has Baroque furnishings.

208 The interior of the Diet is brought to mind by the location of the furniture for the assembly of the provincial court.

209 The Offices of the New Land Rolls with inscriptions and the painted coats-of-arms of the clerks – 16th – 18th century).

210 Detail of copies of the books of the Land Rolls, so-called quaterns.

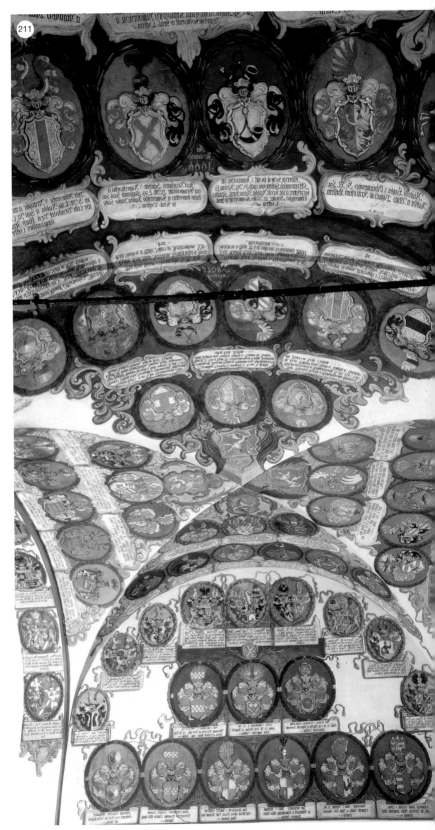

211 The coats-of-arms of the clerks on the walls and vaults of the New Land Rolls were painted according to long-established regulations. Their 16th-century groupings have the form of pyramids whose summit is formed by the emblem of the Czech kingdom.

212 The Riders' Steps were the main entrance to the Vladislav Hall. Low and wide, they made it possible also for horses to enter the hall: proof exists of the fact that tournaments of knights took place in it from time to time. The vault of the Riders' Steps, which manifests the decorativeness and playfulness of the Late Gothic as well as precise stonemason's work, is exceptionally remarkable.

213 **The Basilica of St. George** faces the square U svatého Jiří with its Early Baroque façade, behind which its typical white Romanesque twin steeples of cretaceous marly limestone rise. The neighbouring Neo-Gothic building of the New Deanery was built after a project by J. Mocker.

214 From the square it is possible to view **the eastern end of St. Vitus's Cathedral.** The lower part up to the roof of the chapel is the work of Matthias of Arras, the upper part, including the supporting system, having been built by Peter Parler.

215 At the turn of the 19th and 20th centuries **the interior of St. George's Basilica** was reconstructed into its supposed original form, but a large part of the unviolated original structures and decorations has been preserved.

216 The eastern part of St. George's **Basilica** with the choir and the main apse, below which a Romanesque crypt of the 12th century is concealed. The tombstones in front of the staircase and the entrance to the crypt mark the graves of the Přemyslid princes. The stone tomb situated wholly on the right with a painted, nouse-like extension piece belongs to Vratislav I, who founded the original church consecrated to St. George about 920.

217 St. George's Convent, founded in 973, has been preserved in its Early Baroque form, which it acquired as the result of its reconstruction in the latter half of the 17th century. In the course of the years 1969 to 1975 it was reconstructed in order to house a permanent exposition of works of art from the collections of the National Gallery.

218 An important part of St. George's Basilica is represented by St. Ludmila's Chapel. The tomb of Princess Ludmila stands in the centre of the chapel decorated with a Baroque marble balustrade with a forged grille.

219 The tiny houses in the Golden **Lane** (Zlatá ulička). **In 1597 the Castle marksmen were permitted** to build little houses in the recesses below the bearing arches of the fortifications in the sector from the tower Daliborka to St. George's Convent. They were built on the basis of a special document issued by the Emperor Rudolph II in 1597. A safety passage, intended for the marksmen using firearms, runs along the wall above the tiny houses. Some of the loopholes were even equipped with rotating wooden

drums, which afforded the defenders of the Castle the maximum protection against the artillery of the enemy.

220 The Golden Lane has an inimitable atmosphere also at night.

221 From Jiřská Street a stone gateway leads to the area of the Old Burgrave's House. The coats-of-arms above it bring the four supreme burgraves of the 17th and 18th centuries to mind.

222 The building of the Old Burgrave's House was lent its Renaissance appearance by the reconstruction which G. Ventura carried out in 1555. The building is of much older origin, however, and it even contains the lower part of one of the Romanesque steeples. In the 14th century Charles IV lived here.

223 The building of **Lobkovitz Palace** reaches as far as the very eastern gate of the Castle. At the turn of the 15th and 16th centuries several houses occupied its site and after the mid–16th century the lords of Pernštejn built an imposing palace here. One century later the Lobkovitz family had it reconstructed into its present likeness. The photograph shows one of the three stucco and painted Early Baroque ceilings which have been preserved on the first floor of the palace.

224

227

224 The Black Tower (Černá věž) is now the only preserved and visible tower of the Romanesque fortifications of Prague Castle. The Renaissance gate in its close vicinity leads to Opyš, from where there is a fine view of the city.. On the left the corner of Lobkovitz Palace.

225 The southern façade of the former Institute of Gentlewomen and Plečnik's observation pavilion called Bellevue in the Garden on the Ramparts. The balcony projections are mostly remainders of the towers of former Rožmberk Palace.

226 The lower parts of the turrets of the Romanesque fortifications have been well-preserved in the southern courtyard of the Royal Palace, which is accessible from the Garden on the Ramparts. The complicated process of development of the building is clearly to be seen from the narrow space enclosed by the high southern façade of the palace proper and the Theresian wing (on the right).

227 One of the small structures designed by J. Plečnik for the southern gardens of Prague Castle is this slender cretaceous marly limestone pyramid near the big observation terrace.

225

226

228

228 A number of statues from the workshop of the sculptor M. B. Braun can be seen in lower-situated Hartig Garden. Above, on the supporting wall, is the Small Belvedere designed by J. Plečnik.

229 **The view of the historic part of Prague** from the path running through the southern gardens constantly changes. The photograph shows the view between the column of the small pavilion called the Small Belvedere (Malý Belvedér) of St. Nicholas's Church in the Little Quarter.

230 The huge bowl in the centre of the Garden of Paradise (Rajská zahrada) was hewn from a single block of Mrákotín granite. It ranks among J. Plečnik's modifications of the years 1920 to 1927.

231 The entrance portal to the Garden of Paradise above the mouth of the New Castle Steps (Nové zámecké schody).

232 The Royal Summer Palace,
otherwise Queen Anne's Summer Palace, was built at the eastern end of the
Royal Garden (Královská zahrada) to
the order of Ferdinand I. Italian bricklayers along with masons erected a remarkable – purely Italian – building
richly decorated with stone reliefs.
The upper floor and the original roof
in the shape of a reversed ship's keel
date in the latter half of the 16th century, being the work of H. Tirol and B.
Wolmut. The wooden structure of the
truss and the copper covering are for
the greater part original. During the
reign of Joseph II an artillery laboratory was established in the summer
palace and it was not until 1836 that
its military users were forced to leave
the building. The summer palace was
then renewed and adapted for exhibition purposes.

233 One of the reliefs on the façade
of the Royal Summer Palace with Ferdinand I and Anne Jagiello.

234 The Singing Fountain in front of
the Royal Summer Palace gained its
name from the sound which originates
when the water hits the lower bronze
bowl. It was cast by T. Jaroš in the

years 1564 to 1568. It was set in place in 1569 and became the centre of the separately designed garden area (giardinetto), separated from the summer palace by the original wall. The layout of the giardinetto was renewed closely before World War II and again in the Fifties.

235 The group of statues Night (now in front of the Ball-games Hall) is the work of the prominent sculptor of the Czech Baroque M. B. Braun. Another group of statues, called Day, was destroyed by Prussian artillery in 1757.

236 The Ball-games Hall in the Royal Garden, built by B. Wolmut from 1567 to 1569. Its northern façade is covered with very rich graffito dec-

oration with ornamental areas and allegorical figures in the gussets above the arches. The Ball-games Hall was also placed at the disposal of the army during the reign of Joseph II, being converted into a storehouse. On the last day of World War II it was hit by artillery fire and severely damaged. It was renewed in 1952.

237 The garden on the terrace of the Riding-school is of quite recent origin, having been laid out in 1952 on the roof of the then built garages. Originally there was an open-air summer riding-school here which could be seen from the observation gallery of the Riding-school.

238 View from the Castle through the street U Prašného mostu. This part of the northern foreground behind Stag Ditch was once reserved rather for out-buildings and other facilities (an enclosure for carpenters and building workers, a pond, a pheasantry) and the breeding of rare animals (the Lions' Court).

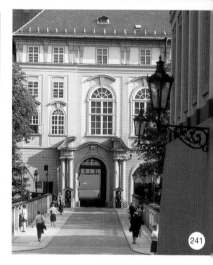

239 From the Royal Garden an unusual view of St. Vitus's Cathedral and the northern fortifications of Prague Castle with the huge cannon tower called Mihulka, also called the Powder Tower, can be seen.

240 View from the upper part of Stag Ditch of the northern wing with the entrance gate to the Castle. The original natural gorge of the little Brusnice River protected Prague Castle on the northern side. During the reign of Ferdinand I it was spanned by a bridge and in the course of the period of rule of Rudolph II it was converted into an enclosure for deer. The slopes were kept in a bare state during the time in which Stag Ditch served a defence purpose. During the Theresian reconstruction the bridge was replaced with a huge embankment.

241 The Pacassi Gate on the site of an older entrance, which originally led to a real bridge spanning Stag Ditch.

242 A changing of the guard ceremony takes place on the stroke of every hour.

243 Plečnik's footpath passing along the façade of the northern wing above Stag Ditch runs from the Garden on the Bastion to the Powder Bridge (Prašný most).

244 The huge cones in the balustrade of Plečnik's footpath are of artificial stone.

245 The Garden on the Bastion (Zahrada Na baště) with the entrance portico of the Spanish Hall. The garden was subjected to modifications in 1930.

246 Plečnik's circular staircase connects the Fourth Courtyard with the higher situated Garden on the Bastion.

V. THE LITTLE QUARTER (MALÁ STRANA)

In 1257 Přemysl Otakar II founded a new town on the left bank of the Vltava, immediately below the Castle. He summoned a German population here and granted it the North German Magdeburg town right. Later this settlement was given the name the Lesser Town (Menší Město) in contradistinction to the Greater Town (Větší město) of Prague as the Old Town was then called.

Otakar's Lesser Town was really small, not much bigger than present Malostranské Square with adjoining blocks of houses, but it was a royal town, which was called the Little Quarter from the 15th century. The area behind the walls of the Lesser Town, which Charles IV later had repaired and enlarged, was far from being unsettled. The communities Na Písku, Trávník, Nebovidy, Obora and particularly the fairly large village Újezd existed on it. Charles IV incorporated them all in the shell of the new walls and permanently connected them with the towns of Prague.

The Little Quarter fortification system had several gates. We are best acquainted with their appearance by the smaller Little Quarter Bridge Tower, which was a part of the fortifications and which has been preserved almost in its original form.

True, the Little Quarter was a royal town, but it did not wholly belong to the king. The plots of land here were owned by the Maltese knights, the archbishop of Prague, the nuns of St. George's Convent, the supreme burgrave, the Thomas and Strahov Monasteries and the Old Town citizens.

The centre of the Little Quarter was a square, which began to be called Malostranské náměstí (Little Quarter Square). It was divided into two parts from the very beginning: an upper and a lower part. The dividing line was formed by St. Wenceslas' Rotunda, the predecesor of present St. Nicholas' Church.

One of the oldest buildings in the Little Quarter was the bishop's court, founded in the late 12th century at the place, where Judith's Bridge linked up with the Little Quarter. Until then the bishops had resided at the Castle, but towards the end of the 12th century they transferred their residence to this seat. About 1263 the court was repaired and at the time of Bishop Jan IV of Dražice it was reconstructed and artistically decorated. Preserved in the court in the house At the Three Golden Bells (U tří zlatých zvonů) at No. 16/47 in Mostecká Street is a Gothic tower, once the gate of the former bishop's court. The coats-of-arms of Jan IV. of Dražice and Archbishop Jan Očko of Vlašim are well-preserved on its façade. The Church of Our Lady Below the Chain is another monument of the medieval Little Quarter. It is now partly Gothic and partly Baroque, but it was once a triple-naved Romanesque building built by the monastery of the Maltese Knights of St. John. One of the most important architectural complexes in the Little Quarter at that time was the monastery with the Church of St. Thomas, whose presbytery was consecrated in 1315. The monastery was inhabited by the Augustians – hermits who set out from here as missionaries at the time of Charles IV.

Charles IV increased the size of the Little Quarter several times and newly fortified it. Practically the whole of the cretaceous marly limestone Hunger Wall, a part of Charles's fortification, has been preserved. The medieval phase of development of the Little Quarter nearly disappeared during the Hussite wars and especially during the great fire of 1541. As regards historic buildings, the Little Quarter is strongly Baroque.

Prague's largest Baroque buildings include the palaces of the newly rich military commanders Albrecht of Valdštejn and Michna of Vacín.

Albrecht of Valdštejn, Duke of Frýdlant and the imperial generalissimo, wholly transformed the original petty bourgeoisie Little Quarter with his Little Quarter palace. From 1624 to 1630 he feverishly built a large seat, which was closed to the surrounding world and concentrated round five courtyards and an architecturally laid out garden. The architect A. Spezza connected a sala terrena, built in the style of the Late Italian Renaissance, and the building of a riding-shool closing the area on the eastern side with the building complex.

The Jesuits, who arrived in Prague in 1556, waged a long-term struggle with the Little Quarter community, which obstructed them in their building enterprise. Not until 1625 did the Emperor Ferdinand II approve the handing-over of a church, a school, the priest's house and the office for the head to the order, whose main task was to re-Catholize mainly non-Catholic Prague. The Jesuits gradually purchased several Little Quarter burghers' houses and began to build up a large area for the order. The first architect concerned was G. D. Orsi, whose work was continued after his death by F. Lurago, who from 1680 to 1688 built, as a part of the whole, Baroque St. Wenceslas's Church on the site of a demolished Romanesque rotunda. In 1773 St. Wenceslas's Church was abolished and converted into offices and storehouses and a new church consecrated to St. Nicholas began to originate on the Little Quarter area. The builder of the church was K. Dienzenhofer, its construction being completed by his son K. I. Dienzenhofer. He closed the church and also built its 70-metres high cupola, which was something entirely new in the Prague environment. The most outstanding creative artists participated in the decoration of the exceptional interior of St. Nicholas' Church, the summit of Prague Baroque illusionism.

Churches rank among the most numerous and the most remarkable Baroque buildings and the long series of these Prague edifices was begun with the reconstruction of the former Lutheran Church of the Holiest Trinity into the Church of Our Lady Victorious in Karmelitská Street in the Little Quarter. In 1624 the Carmelites gained it as a reward for the heroism of their general in the Battle on the White Mountain. The church is a monument to this victory and it was therefore consecrated to Our Lady Victorious. On one of its altars there is a small statue of the famous Prague Jesus Child.

The central Church of St. Joseph attached to the monastery of the Carmelites is a unique Baroque building in Prague. It has a striking façade receding from the front of the houses in Josefská Street. It was built from 1687 to 1693 in Belgian Baroque style.

Prague's Early Baroque palaces include, for example, Schönborn Palace in the place called Tržiště (now the seat of the embassy of the U. S.). It was projected by J. B. Santini or G. B. Alliprandi and a well-known garden adjoins it.

The effect of the Grand Prior's Palace, built by B. Scotti, is enhanced by the work of the outstanding Baroque sculptor M. B. Braun. The architect J. B. Santini-Aichl cooperated with sculptors M. B. Braun and F. M. Brokoff in the building of Morzín and Thun Palaces in Nerudova Street.

The most outstanding representative of the latter half of the 18th century was I. J. N. Palliardi, whose small Fürstenberg Garden crowned the development of Prague's Baroque gardens. In 1787 Palliardi rebuilt Ledebour Palace and modified its terraced garden on the southern slope below Prague Castle.

The Neo-Renaissance and the Neo-Baroque of the later half of the 19th century did not have much effect on the Little Quarter. The building of the municipal secondary school and the later „realschule" in Hellichova Street, built after a Neo-Renaissance design by J. Srdínek, is almost unique.

A large Jesuit garden once spread out below Letná Plain, to the east of Klárov. The garden fell into a state of neglect and in 1896 Q. Bělský built a boarding school for children of the nobility on its site. In the period between the two world wars this monumental building was the academic home of university students (the Straka Academy) and it now houses the office of the presidium of the government.

247 Already in the early Middle Ages the separate community Obora with the parish Church of St. John spread out below the Castle. Only the names of the streets have remained of St. John's Church and the cemetery surrounding it. This street, for example, is called John's Hill (Jánský vršek).
248 The House on the corner of Šporkova Street and Jánský vršek, called At the Three Golden Crowns (U tří zlatých korun), dates in the later half of the 18th century.
249 A house in Jánská Street decorated with fine Neo-Renaissance graffiti.
250 Former **Schönborn Palace** is now the seat of the American em-

253

254

bassy. It is an Early Baroque building of 1643 to 1656 whose height was raised in the early 18th century by the addition of gables and dormer windows. Its interior was modified after a plan by G. Santini. The palace is adjoined by a large garden with a Neo-Renaissance glorietto, built after 1650 and ranking among Prague's most beautiful palace gardens.

251 The Casa d'Italia, originally the **Italian Hospital,** was built by Italian immigrants serving at the court of Rudolph II. It is an Early Baroque building with an arcarded courtyard. From 1804 it housed an orphanage and after 1942 it was converted into the social centres of the Italian colony in Prague. The hospital Church of St. Charles Borromaeus is Baroque with 19th-century modifications.

252 View of Hradčany from Vlašská Street. On the right is the well-known panorama of Hradčany with St. Vitus' Cathedral and on the left is the huge Renaissance Schwarzenberg Palace, decorated with rustic graffiti.

253 The renewed German-Czech street sign on the façade of the palace of the American embassy recalls the fact that Italian immigrants, who had their own hospital here, lived nearby in the 17th century.

254 Baroque **Lobkovitz Palace** originally belonged to Přehořovský of Kasejovice. It is now the seat of the embassy of the Federal Republic of Germany. It was built after plans by G. B. Alliprandi in 1707 and in 1769 I. Palliardi added another storey. The palace has a large Baroque garden, converted into a natural park in the late 18th century. Access to the garden is gained through a grille gate whose pillars bear groups of statues The Abduction of Proserpine and The Abduction of Orithyia of 1720.

petual Aid, built by the Theatines, and former Thun Hohenštejn Palace.

258 Let us continue on our way... The red house in the background is on the New Castle Steps.

259 The Provincial Diet of the Czech Kingdom assembled in Sněmovní Street and from 1918 the supreme constitutional organs of the republic did so. A memorial tablet reminds us that the Czechoslovak Republic was proclaimed here on 28 October, 1918.

260 The Czech Diet, formerly Thun Palace, was originally Baroque, but in 1801 it was wholly rebuilt after a fire in 1794. Its present façade dates from that time.

255 There are many little streets and passageways below Prague Castle. This one is called Thunovská.

256 Former Thun Palace now belongs to the British Embassy. It was built after plans by A. Lurago from 1716 to 1727. The Romantic Gothic courtyard wing dates in the mid–19th century. W. A. Mozart and his wife Constance lived in the palace during their first visit to Prague in January 1787. In the foreground is the silhouette of a bust of W. Churchill with the inscription „Determination in war, resistance in defeat, magnanimity in victory, good will in peace" on the pedestal.

257 These steps lead to the Castle. They begin in Nerudova Street between the Church of Our Lady of Per-

261 and **262** **The New Castle Steps** lead from the Castle to Klárov. On the New Castle Steps there are several fine Renaissance buildings: At St. John Nepomuk's (U sv. Jana Nepomuckého), At the Cross (U kříže), At the Pelican (U pelikána) and At the Golden Lion (U zlatého lva).

263 The Memorial of the Victims of Communism by Olbram Zoubek is placed at the foothill of Petřín.

264 The Early Gothic Church of St. John „Na prádle" is one of the oldest churches in the Little Quarter. In 1520 the Czech humanist and master of free arts, the dean of the faculty of Charles University and a supporter of the Union of Brethren Viktorin Kornel of Všehrdy was buried in it in 1520.

265 **The Umělecká beseda** society organized Czech cultural life already in the 19th century. In 1926 it moved to the Little Quarter and since then its interiors have been the scene of many exhibitions, concerts and theatre performances.

266 House No. 532/11 in Říční Street was inhabited by the family of Dr. Antonín Čapek, his elder son Josef and his younger son Karel.

267 The evidently renowned Czech photographer J. Sudek had his studio in the street **Na Újezdě.**

268 The streets Újezd and Karmelitská. Újezd was named after an old community incorporated into the Little Quarter and Karmelitská after the monastery of the Mendicant Carmelites who settled here by the Church of Our Lady Victorious from the mid–17th century.

269 After Valdštejn, Pavel Michna of Vacín was the richest aristocrat in Bohemia. He increased his property with confiscations after the Battle on the White Mountain. The Michna's beautified this house until it became a palace. In 1921 the Czech Sokol Community made it its centre. Standing in the courtyard is a statue of the founder of this physical culture organization Dr. M. Tyrš.

270 Marie Manrique de Lara, wife of Vratislav of Pernštejn, brought the wax statue of the Jesus Child to Bohemia. Due to the influence of St. Theresa in the 17th century its renown spread throughout Spain. This statue, performing miracles, was later presented by M. de Lara's daughter Polyxena of Lobkovitz to the Carmelite monastery attached to Our Lady Victorious. And the Child Jesus began to perform miracles in Prague.

271 Terraced **Vrtba Garden** is the work of the architect F. M. Kaňka of about 1720.

272 The Maltese-Johannite order developed from the brotherhood of Italian merchants who about 1040 founded a hospital in Jerusalem for the care of pilgrims to the Holy Sepulchre. In 1334 the Emperor Charles IV bestowed the feoff of Malta on the Johannite order. From then on it was the main seat of their Grand Master. The Maltese knights were established in Bohemia during the reign of Vladislav II in the years 1156 to 1159 and their oldest commenda originated just here in the Little Quarter. It was the main seat of the supreme representative of the Bohemian Maltese province. The building in the photo is **the convent of the order of Maltese Knights.**

273 **The House at the Golden Unicorn** (U zlatého jednorožce) in the Little Quarter was once a foremost Prague hotel and wayside inn. In 1796 L. van Beethoven stayed here.

274 This memorial tablet with a relief portrait of 1927 recalling the sejour of L. van Beethoven in Prague is the work of the leading Czech sculptor and medallist O. Španiel.

275 **The Church of Our Lady Below the Chain** brings the ancient Maltese monastery founded in the 12th century to mina. It is a very big, uncompleted triple-naved church of the Maltese knights. Its ancientness is documented by its Gothic façade with huge fortress towers. It was barocized by C. Lurago in the 17th century.

276 This **group statues of St. John the Baptist** with three angels was created in the square Maltezské náměstí on the basis of an order from the Maltese Prior by F. M. Brokoff from 1714 to 1715. In the background can be seen the house At the Painters (U malířů) with a characteristic Little Quarter restaurant.

277 **The Baroque palace of the Maltese Grand Prior.** The decoration of the portal is from M. Braun's workshop.

278 **The arcading of the Conservatoire and the Jan Deyl School for Tuners** (formerly Deyl's Institute for the Blind).

279 **The palace of the Japanese embassy** in the square Maltézské náměstí is a Baroque building of the latter half of the 17th century.

280 **Nostic Palace** is a Baroque building of about 1660. Its former owner Count F. A. Nostic-Rieneck was a keen patron of sciences and arts. Leading scholars gathered in his palace and their meetings gave rise to the Royal Society or Sciences, later the Czech Academy of Sciences.

278

279

280

281 Kampa Island is one of the most beautiful places in Prague. It lies almost in the centre of the city and abounds in greenery. The Vltava and the Devil's Stream flow round it. One of its walls in Velkopřevorské Square was originally decorated with a portrait of John Lennon. However, this decoration was destroyed by flooding in 2002 and newly made later on.

282 Baroque Buquoy Palace is the seat of the French embassy. It dates in 1719 and was rebuilt in the late Thirties of the 18th century. Its rear tract gained its present appearance in 1896 (architect J. Schulz). The staircase is Neo-Renaissance.

283 The portal of **Small Buquoy Palace** at the beginning of Lázeňská Street.

284 Renaissance **Grand Prior's Mill** with a wooden mill wheel with bottom drive is one of the last water mills on the Devil's Stream. It remembers the late 16th century.

285 This charming Classical building on the bank of the Devil's Stream was adapted into a flat and studio by the illustrator of books of fairy-tales and creator of puppet and animated films **Jiří Trnka** (1912–1969). In the latter half of the 19th century the house was owned by the founder of the theatre in Smíchov, director and teacher of many Czech actors P. Švanda of Semčice.

286 The philologist and patriarch of Czech Slav studies J. Dobrovský (1753–1829) lived in the garden house on **Kampa Island.** Count B. J. Nostic had it converted into an atractive dwelling. Standing in front of the

house, whose garden is a part of the large park, is a memorial to Dobrovský, the work of T. Seidan of 1891.

287 The house At the Blue Fox (U modré lišky) on Kampa Island was marked by this cunning little beast of prey already in 1664, when it was rebuilt and in essence gained its present appearance. An old legend tell us that a gamekeeper's lodge once stood here.

288 This gate leads us to **Kampa Island.** The lower branch of the Devil's Stream flowing round it lends this place the character of Venice.

289 The waters of the Vltava and the Devil's Stream drove **Sova's Mills** from time immemorial. The original building was rebuilt on order of Meda Mládková for a purpose of the Gallery of Modern Arts. Particularly the pictures by F. Tichý and F. Kupka can be seen here.

290 Early Baroque **Lichtenštejn Palace** on Kampa was rebuilt in Classical style. It has its original portal.

291 Since 1599 pottery markets have taken place in the characteristic little square called Na Kampě. Jugs and mugs from Kampa became typical Prague souvenirs.

292 Close by Charles Bridge stands a house with a balcony. Below its sable there is an ancient painting of the Virgin, allegedly brought here by the Vltava during a flood.

293 Memorial tablets and busts on a wall of the garden house on Kampa inform us that the Prague historian Z. Wirth (1878–1961) and the actor, dramatist, writer and film scenarist J. Werich (1905–1980) lived here.

294 Charles Bridge is the fourth stone bridge in Bohemia. Charles IV had it built, entrusting the plans and supervision of its construction to the outstanding architect P. Parler. There are Baroque sculptures on it.

295 The historic centre of Prague can be reached by boat. In this way you can get to know the river and its islands, embankments and bridges.

296 The Baroque **Church of St. Joseph** with a façade articulated by embossed half-columns and pillasters of the Netherlandish type is decorated with sculptures by M. Jackel. Inside there is a painting by P. Brandl.

297 Josefská Street. In the background St. Thomas's Church, a combination of the Gothic and the Baroque.

298 This group of statues of St. Hubert and a stag with a cross between its antlers was hewn on this house in Tomašská Street by F. M. Brokoff in 1726.

299 From 1624 to 1630 A. Spezza and G. Sebregondi of Lombardy built this large palace, concentrated round an architecturally laid out garden and five courtyards, for Albrecht of Valdštejn. The photo shows its façade. Valdštejn Garden is known for de Vries's bronze statues of classical gods which were taken to Stockholm by the Swedes in 1848 as war booty. The gem of the garden is the Renaissance sala terrena, built by A. Spezza of Italy.

300 Ledebour Palace in Valdštejnské Square was adapted in 1787 by I. Palliardi. Near it stands the Renaissance house At the Three Roses (U tří růží). Behind the palace is a terraced garden.

301 Valdštejnská Street. In the foreground is Kolovrat Palace, built in Late Baroque style by I. Palliardi. In the background is Palffy Palace. From the 13th century to 1623 Písecká Gate, one of the gates of the Little Quarter's fortifications, stood in its middle.

302 **Fürstenberg Palace** was built by an unknown architect in the mid–18th century for Count V. K. Netolický. In 1822 it became the property or the Fürstenberg princes. One of them, Karel Egon, formed a centre of German and Czech culture here.

303 Former **Klar's Institute for the Blind** is a Classical building of 1836 to 1846. Its gable bears a relief by J. Max: Tobias Restores His Father's Sight.

304 **The Hoffmeister Hotel,** the work of architect P. Keil of 1991 to 1993, is one of the largest post-war Little Quarter buildings. This sensitively conceived reconstruction of old houses in the bend of Chotkova Street gave rise to a harmonious complex of modern buildings which soon became a part of its environment.

305 Classical **Richter's summer palace** was once the vinicultural house of the St. Wenceslas Vineyard which is said to have been founded and cultivated by Prince Vaclav himself. Behind the wall the charming little street Na Opyši rises to the Castle.

306 The group of statues J. A. Komenský (Comenius) Takes Farewell of His Country was created by the sculptor, sketcher, graphic artist and architect F. Bílek.

307 **Bruska Gate** is a remainder of Prague's Baroque fortifications. It was especially useful during the wars in the reign of Maria Theresa.

VI. THE JEWISH TOWN

In 63 B. C. the Romans conquered Palestine. In the year zero Christ was born and thirty-three years later crucified. In 70 A. D., after the defeat of the Jews, the Roman legions destroyed the temple in Jerusalem and the Jews were driven from their homeland. From then on their ranks were dispersed,, first of all round the Mediterranean Sea and later throughout the whole world, including Bohemia. Their diligent and cultural presence in Prague is documented in written records from the mid-10th century and it merges with the very beginnings of the town. As they were able merchants and highly needed craftsmen they enjoyed the same privileges as, for example, German entrepreneurs in the outer bailey of the castle of the princes. Let it be recalled that Prague inherited three cultures – the Czech, the German and the Jewish ones.

However, already in the late 11th century Prague was also infected by the malignant European disease called anti-Semitism. In the years 1096 to 1098 Prague was affected by the first crusade heading for Palestine and it was a witness to the first anti-Jewish manifestations. The Jews thus preferred to emigrate, but Prince Břetislav II (1092–1100) rid them of their property. True, the ruler granted the Jews various privileges, but they had to pay dearly for them.

In 1215 the anti-Jewish ideology was asserted at the 4th Council in Rome at the time of Pope Innocence III. The Jews were not allowed to own land, to work in the fields or to practice crafts. And so they began to concern themselves with financial affairs, which meant loans and usury. For Christians this was a mark of immorality.

Contacts of the Jews with the rest of the population were restricted and the Jews had to wear a special symbol or garment distinguishing them from the rest of the world and so they withdrew into ghettos out of both necessity and self-defence in order to preserve their religion and traditions beyond the city walls.

In the course of the development of Prague the once scattered Jewish communities of merchants and craftsmen in the Little Quarter, below Vyšehrad and in the vicinity of present Old Town Square ceased to exist. When King Václav I had the Old Town fortified with walls before 1241 the Jews gradually concentrated round the Old-New (Staronová) Synagogue, this giving rise to the Jewish Town, which later became a ghetto with its own walls and six gates.

Only after many centuries, from the latter half of the 19th century, did the Jews gain the same rights as the other inhabitants of Prague. They acquired freedom of movement and residence and access to education and they left the ghetto. In the late 19th century the Jewish Town became a quarter of the poor of Prague. True, the ancient and bizarre, but unhygienic and confined environment did not meet the demands of the modern development of the town. At the turn of the 19th and 20th centuries the ghetto was wholly demolished, romantic and Art Nouveau blocks and apartment houses springing up on its site. However, the synagogues, the Jewish Town Hall and the cemetery remained.

In 1254 the Czech king Přemysl Otakar II granted the Jew's privileges as direct subjects of the king. He afforded them protection and permitted them to engage in financial affairs. He also forbid violent measures to be taken against their property and customs. Přemysl Otakar II was able to base this decision on the bull issued by Pope Innocence IV who, contrary to his predecessor, manifested solidarity towards the Jews. However, when they needed money the kings themselves took it from rich Jews by force. In 1296 Václav II demanded a ransom after capturing Prague's Jews. The father of the illustrious Emperor Charles IV, King John of Luxembourg, imprisoned the Jewish board of representatives in 1336 and took away everything of value from the Old-New Synagogue. In 1385 King Václav IV imprisoned the Jewish elders and confiscated their property. However, the Jews always succeeded in renewing it and their culture remained unviolated.

The poet and rabbi Avigdor Kara survived the pogrom of Easter 1389, which left 3,000 men, women and children dead. Avigdor's elegy is still read on the Day of Conciliation in the Old-New Synagogue. Other pogroms took place also in later years (1422–1744). The Jews were often banished from Prague, but they returned.

In the late 17th century the Jesuits exerted pressure on the Jews in an effort to make them become Christians. Nineteen-years-old Simon Abeles had himself christened and was immediately murdered for doing so. In a mock trial in 1694 an attempt was made to prove that the murderers came from the ghetto. However, in the same year the new building of the Klaus Synagogue was completed on a site next to the cemetery, where three buildings of 1571 had once stood: a synagogue, a ritual bath and a Talmudic school. These were destroyed by fire in 1689.

Not until the Tolerance Patent was issued in 1781 by the Emperor Joseph II did the position of the Jews in Prague improve. Equal rights were granted to all religions, although the Catholics continued to enjoy certain privileges. The Jews gained real equal rights de jure on the basis of the first Austrian constitution of 1848 and de facto after 1867 with the new establishment of the monarchy. In 1861 the Jewish Town ceased to be a ghetto and became Prague's fifth town with the name of Josefov to commemorate the tolerant sovereign Joseph II, who also visited the ghetto during his reign (1780–1790).

The cultural public was not satisfied with the liquidation of the Prague ghetto in the late 19th century, wanting it to be preserved as a historic monument. Engineers, hygiene workers and the Jews themselves supported the clearance work, however. Rich Jews built new houses beyond the boundaries of the ghetto, or in the newly developing town quarters, for example, in Vinohrady. And thus at the turn of the century 300 houses and over 30 little streets disappeared. The Jewish Town Hall, the Old-New and High Synagogues and the Old Jewish Cemetery were preserved in the centre of the former ghetto. The Maisel and Spanish Synagogues were rebuilt.

In all 14 synagogues have remained in Prague, some of them being situated in outlying districts. The most recent and the most important of them is the Jubilee Synagogue (1906), built beyond the original Jewish quarter in Jeruzalemská Street near Wilson Station of the present.

There are about 12.000 gravestones in the Old Jewish Cemetery. Burials took place in it from 1438 to 1787, when cemeteries, and not only the Jewish ones, were not allowed to remain inside the town for health reasons. The first gravestones are of sandstone, later ones being of marble. The quadratic Hewbrew script on them is supplemented with sculptured pictures expressing the name, origin or profession of the deceased. Hands held out in blessing mean that the deceased was an ancestor of the old biblical priests of the Cohen family.

The great Prague rabbi Jehuda Low ben Becalel (1512–1609) was an outstanding personality. He was a brilliant teacher, organizer and writer and a legend tells us that he created Golem of unimaginable strength. The myth about Golem is one of Prague's most interesting legends and it interests also modern writers due to its ever topical theme: how to master the forces thought-up by Man, but which are stronger than Man himself. Jacob Apell was a high official during the reign of Prince Vladislav I (1109–1117) and during the Thirty Years War Jacob Bašev of Trauenberg (1580–1634) was, as the first Jew in the history of the Hapsburg monarchy to receive the honour, raised to the aristocracy.

In the early 20th century renown was gained for Prague by Jewish writers who wrote in German: Franz Werfel, Max Brod and especially Franz Kafka, who was born on the border of the Old Town and the Jewish ghetto.

During World War II 360,000 Czechoslovak citizens died, at least 200,000 of them being Jews who were murdered by the Nazis. Nowadays Prague's Jewish community has about 1,000 members. According to the census of the population of 1991 218 persons in the Czech Republic avow Jewish nationality, 1,392 of them avowing the Jewish religion. The seat of the Federation of the Jewish Religious Communities of the Czech Republic is situated in the a few steps away are the Old-New and the High Synagogues and particularly the Old Jewish Cemetery.Jewish Town Hall in Maislova Street in Prague 1. Here it is possible to eat kosher meals in a period-furnished dining-room and just

The Old Jewish Cemetery in Prague is one of the best-preserved and the oldest Jewish cemeteries in the world in general and apart from its immense value as regards knowledge and its historical importance it has a special and inimitable charm and atmosphere. The visitor walks through an oasis of quiet and memories under large trees and above all he is amazed by the surprising density and stratification of the gravestones, each one of which is an original work of art. The Jewish cemetery could not permanently expand in the closely demarcated ghetto and so it was necessary to stratify the graves and also preserve the gravestones of previously deceased persons in their places. There are more graves than gravestones here and perhaps no one has succeeded in counting them precisely to date. There are about 12,000 gravestones, the first of which dates in 1439. The last burial took place here in 1787. There was an even older Jewish cemetery in the region of present Vladislavova Street in the New Town. However, it ceased to exist and the discovered stones were transferred to the Old Jewish Cemetery.

We can set out on a visit to the Old Jewish Cemetery from Široká Street through the court of the Pinkas Synagogue, but it is better to pass through the gate between the building of the Burial Brotherhood of Prague and the Klaus Synagogue, i.e. from the street called U starého hřbitova. All the gravestone are interesting for something or other, but attention should be paid to the most outstanding of them. (Their location corresponds to the numbers in the plan.)

1. Reliefs of a bear and a lion with medical instruments indicate the graves of physicians of the late 17th century. 2. Gothic stones transferred here from the abolished cemetery in the New Town. 3. „Nefele" hillock (the Hebrew word „nefele" means miscarriage). Children who were born dead were buried here and later accumulated remains and stones from abolished graves were also placed here. 4. The sandstone gravestone of Aharon Mesullam Horovic (†1545). A family synagogue was established in the house of the Hořovský family and from the late 16th century it was known as the Pinkas Synagogue. 5. The rabbi, poet and scholar Ávigdor Kara (†1439). The valuable original gravestone is deposited in the Klaus Synagogue and its a precise copy is located here. 6. David Cans (†1613), symbols of the Jewish star and goose. 7. Mordechaj Kohen (†1592) and his son Becalel (†1589) of the renowned Gersonid family of printers. 8. The sarcophagus of David Oppenheim (†1736), a Moravian and later Prague and provincial rabbi. 9. The tomb (†1601) of the Jewish mayor Mordechai Maisel. 10. Rabbi Low (†1609) and his wife Perl (†1610). 11. Selomo Efraim Luntsic, from 1604 the chief rabbi. 12. The tomb of Hendl Baševi ranks among the most beautiful gravestones (†1628).

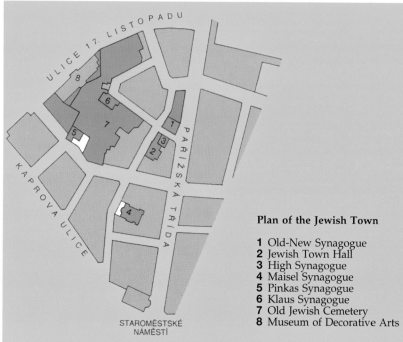

Plan of the Jewish Town

1 Old-New Synagogue
2 Jewish Town Hall
3 High Synagogue
4 Maisel Synagogue
5 Pinkas Synagogue
6 Klaus Synagogue
7 Old Jewish Cemetery
8 Museum of Decorative Arts

308 This aerial photograph shows the location of the Jewish ghetto up to the late 19th century. The bizarre little streets have been replaced with wide ones (on the left Kaprova Street, on the right Pařížská Street running to Svatopluk Čech Bridge). Only the synagogue, Jewish Town Hall and the Old Jewish Cemetery (the green trees on the left of the centre) remained after the clearance activity carried out in the quarter called Josefov.

309 The statue of Moses (1905) by František Bílek. It portrays Moses in a state of exhaustion after returning from Mount Sinai. This Art Nouveau work stands in the small park in front of the Old-New Synagogue at the place where Maiselova Street joins Pařížská Street. During the war the statue was destroyed by the Nazis and a copy of it was unveiled in 1948.

310 The clock on the tower of the Jewish Town Hall has measured time since the latter half of the 17th century. The present appearance of the tower originated after a fire in 1754. The hands on the dial with Jewish figures turn backwards in accordance with the way in which a Hebrew text is read. However, they show the same time. This speciality captivated the French poet Apollinaire and it became the symbol of Jewish Prague in his modern poetry.

311 The core of the Jewish town has always been the three buildings standing near one another here. They survived the clearance of the ghetto at the end of the century. The Town Hall of the Jewish Town (with a clock) of the latter half of the 16th century, rebuilt by J. Schlessinger before 1763. The Town Hall and the neighbouring High Synagogue were founded by the mayor of the Jewish Town Mordechaj Maisel in 1601. Maiselova Street was named after him. The Old-New Synagogue (brick gable in foreground) dates in the mid-13th century.

312 The building of the High Synagogue (completed in 1568), once formed a part of the Jewish Town Hall.

313 The Klaus Synagogue (1694) on the site of a smaller synagogue, a Talmudistic school and liturgical bath existed which were all victims of a fire.

314 The Maisel Synagogue was built on the basis of a privilege granted by the Emperor Rudolph II to the Jewish builder Juda Corefe de Herz (1590–1592) as Mordechaj Maisel's private synagogue.

315 The Spanish Synagogue (1868, V. I. Ullmann and J. Niklas) was built in Moorish style on the site once occupied by the oldest synagogue in the Jewish Town.

316 The Pinkas Synagogue is a Late Gothic building with a single nave with a net vault. It was built on the site of an older house of prayer (1492) by Mešulam Hořovský (1535). Since its reconstruction (1950–1959) it has housed the Memorial to Jewish Victims of Nazism.

317 The inscriptions of the names of 77,297 Czech and Moravian Jewish victims of Nazi racism during World War II. Their names were inscribed manually on the walls inside the Pinkas Synagogue by the painters J. John and V. Boštík. The names of the victims are arranged according to the individual communities and family names.

318 The building of the Jewish Museum stands in Jáchymova Street connecting Maiselova Street with Pařížská Street. It has accumulated relics and documents pertaining to the Jewish settlement since 1906.

315

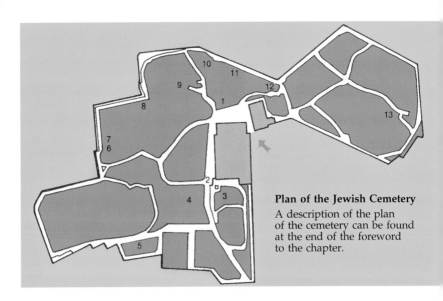

Plan of the Jewish Cemetery

A description of the plan of the cemetery can be found at the end of the foreword to the chapter.

319 **The new Hall of Mourning of the Burial Society** next to the entrance to the Old Jewish Cemetery. This cretaceous marly limestone building by J. Gerstl (1906–1908) has a Neo-Romanesque appearance and burial processions took place here only to the early 20th century.

320 **Fragments of old Gothic tombstones** (14th century) by the entrance to the cemetery. They were removed from the older Jewish cemetery in the New Town.

321 **These tombstones** date from 1439–1787 and 12,000 of them have been counted. They are inscribed with Hebrew quadratic script. With the development of history the initially simple inscriptions changed into poetic chronicles about the deceased. Stone slabs made way, especially in the Baroque period, for sculptured works **(322)**. In the background the Klaus Synagogue. The reliefs of things or animals on the gravestones stylize the name or origin of the deceased. For example, an ewer **(323)** means the Levi family. The shield-bearing lion **(324)** marks the grave of Hendel Bashevi (1628), the charitable daughter of a prominent family. She is the only woman to be buried separately here and she has her own gravestone. The oldest gravestones **(325)** include that of the mayor of the Jewish Town Mordechaj Maisel (1601) and the greatest attention is aroused by the tomb **(326)** of Jehuda ben Bacalel, called Rabbi Low, the creator of Golem, and his wife Perl.

327 This **bust of Franz Kafka** marks the place where the great Prague writer of the German language and Jewish culture was born (K. Hladík 1967)

328 **The building of the so-called new prelature** next to St. Nicholas's Church in Old Town Square. A gateway leading to the ghetto and the house called At the Golden Face (U zlaté tváře), where Franz Kafka was born on 3. 7. 1883. His family house and the gateway disappeared during the clearance activity.

329 **The House At the Minute** (Dům U minuty), originally called the House at the White Lion, a sculpture of which is situated on the corner. Franz Kafka lived in this enchanting corner between Old Town Square and Small Square (1889–1896).

330 **The white cross** in the paving in front of the Old Town Hall marks the place where 27 leaders of the uprising of the Czech Estates against the Hapsburg Emperor and Czech king were executed on 21. 6. 1621.

331 **The window in the southern wall** of Týn Church through which Franz Kafka observed the interior of the Gothic church with Renaissance tombs and Baroque altars. He lived with his parents in house No. 3 in Celetná Street, originally Romanesque and later modified in Gothic style.

332 **The building of The Workers' Injury Insurance Office for the Czech Kingdom** in the street Na Poříčí, where Franz Kafka worked as a lawyer from 1908 to 1922, when he retired.

333 **Kafka's Monument.** Prague centre was enriched with a new memorial in 2003. Bronze statue of the well-known Jewish writer Franz Kafka, made by Jaroslav Róna, was unveiled nearby the place, where Kafka had been born in 1883 – at Dušní Street. The modern statue should symbolise the atmosphere of Kafka's works.

VII. THE OLD TOWN

In the latter half of the 12th century the communities of merchants below Prague Castle and Vyšehrad lost their importance and the Old Town market-place, now Old Town Square, became the centre of Prague's economic life. The communication axis was formed by the ford across the River Vltava at the place where Manes Bridge now stands. On the right bank of the river routes ran from it to the south, the north and the east and by the main communication of this fork there originated a large marketplace adjoined by the Týn frame merchants' court with the Ungelt custom-house. During the l0th century a community of merchants and several villages with parish churches sprang up in its environs.

In the early 13th century the Old Town merchants built St. Nicholas' Church, which stood roughly in the place now occupied by Dienzenhofer's Baroque church consecrated to the same saint. By the church there was a cemetery, a priest's house and a school. This small town did not have a Town Hall. The councillors assembled in private houses and important matters were discussed in the church. It was finally John of Luxembourg that granted the burghers the right to establish a councillors' house. This purpose was served by the house of Wolfin of Kamene. It stood in the centre of the market-place, present Small Square (Malé náměstí) forming a part of it. Later the Old Town Hall came into being round Wolfin's house.

Standing to the north of the Town Hall was a house owned by the founder of Bethlehem Chapel, a merchant by the name of Kříž, and on the right-hand side of the northern front of the square there was the court of Václav IV's consort, Queen Žofie.

On the eastern side of the square there is a valuable architectural monument in the form of the House at the Stone Bell (Dům U kamenného zvonu), which was one of the most beautiful Old Town buildings already in the 14th century. Former Týn School is situated in its neighbourhood and the fact that it is an ancient building is documented by the remainders of its Romanesque basement and the Early Gothic vault of its arcade.

Týn Church, which was built behind the eastern front of the houses, stands on the site of a small Romanesque church where merchants arriving at the custom-house went. In the 13th century it was replaced with an Early Gothic church which in the 14th century made way for the present Church of Our Lady of Týn.

In the early Middle Ages business life was concentrated in the square of the Old Town, foreign merchants concentrating in the Ungelt and domestic ones in the nearest environs of the Town Hall. Below the Town Hall there were bakers' shops and in the square itself there were stalls where cloth was sold. Furriers sold their goods directly in the Town Hall. Inside the Town Hall block there was a market-place where other goods could be obtained.

In the first half of the 13th century Vladislav II founded Gall's Town (Havelské město) by the southern walls of the Old Town. It stretched from the Coal Market (Uhelný trh) to the Powder Gate (Prašná brána). Originally only St. Gall's Church stood on this large area, being surrounded by a busy market for timber and timber products and a coal market. Later the cloth and fur markets were transferred here from Old Town Square.

Cloth stalls began to be built in Gall's Town in the mid-14th century. Apart from furriers and drapers, tinsmiths also sat in a small part of the little shops, which several centuries later were used for the building of the first permanent theatre in Prague. On the site of the later St. Gall's Monastery, which belonged to the Carmelites, there were bakers' stalls and a communal kitchen. In the mid-13th century Václav I had walls built round the Old Town. They were 10 to 12 metres high and 2 metres thick and they were topped with battlements. In front of them there was a ditch of a width of 15 to 20 metres and a depth of about 8 metres. Small bridges, originally built of wood and later of stone, spanned the ditch and afforded access to the city gates. Towers of a height of 30 metres were built round the whole periphery of the walls. Two or them can still be seen in the block between Národní Street and Bartolomějská Street. Of the gates only Gall's Gate (Havelská brána) has been preserved in its original form. It is concealed in house No. 401 in Rytířská Street to the height of the second floor. The Powder Gate is of later origin. King Vladislav Jagiello founded it on the site of an old medieval gate, the builder being M. Rejsek.

The first stone Romanesque houses, hidden below ground level, could also tell us about life in the outer bailey on the right bank of the Vltava. The Old Town was situated several metres lower than today. When the first weirs were built and the danger of floods increased the people of the Old Town had to raise the level of their town for safety reasons. They achieved this by means of a deposit of earth which was as much as 4 metres in height in some places. As a result the ground-floors of the Romanesque houses found themselves in the cellars of later-built Gothic houses. Whole Romanesque houses have been discovered and carefully restored in the Old Town. Outstanding among them is the court of the lords of Kunštát in Řetězová Street. Another ancient Romanesque monument is the Rotunda of the Holy Rood in Karolína Světlá Street. It has stood here in its unchanged form since the 12th century.

On the right bank of the Vltava, in the north-western corner of the Old Town, Václav I and his sister Anežka founded a convent for the Poor Clares and Princess Anežka was its first Superior. This convent was Prague's first Gothic building. Its core was formed by the long wing of the convent and the double-naved Church of St. Francis. Some time before 1240 the convent was enlarged by a part for monks, this calling for new building activity. In 1261 Přemysl Otakar II had a royal mausoleum, consecrated to Christ the Saviour, built on the convent area. For the construction of this Přemyslid place of burial he summoned a master of the French Gothic whose name is not known, however.

From the late 16th century the Agnes (Anežka) Convent „Na Františku" existed in ruins only. Its renewal was started in 1900, reconstructions being carried out until 1981. An exposition of Czech painting of the 19th century is now installed in the exhibition rooms of the restored convent.

On 21 June, 1621 Old Town Square witnessed some bloody political executions. Ferdinand II had 27 of his religious and political opponents, 27 Protestant aristocrats and burghers, executed here. This event was followed by the confiscation of their property and the outbreak of the destructive Thirty Years War. Prague's impoverished towns had neither the means nor any thought of improving their houses, or beginning new building activity and so the Old Town approximately preserved its appearance of the time before the war. It was not until the end of the 17th century that the foreman mason H. Fritz built the new Church of St. Nicholas after a plan by K. I. Dienzenhofer. This meant the penetration of the Baroque into Prague.

One of the first Baroque buildings in the Old Town is the oval building of the Italian Chapel in the Clementinum, built towards the end of the 16th century. The Clementinum itself ranks among the first Jesuit colleges in Bohemia. The Jesuits, summoned to Prague by Ferdinand I in 1556, initially settled in the Dominican monastery by St. Clement's Church. Not until the beginning of the 18th century was the building-up of their extensive area on the site of the preserved Clementinum started. This historic whole, the biggest in Prague, was built with the constant and generous support of the Hapsburgs throughout long decades, practically up to the time or the abolition of the order in 1773. It stands in a place once occupied by more than 30 houses, gardens, three churches, two streets and one old Dominican monastery. In the course of 150 years a complex of buildings originated round five courtyards with the Church of the Holy Saviour, St. Clement's Church and the Italian Chapel. The building of the college, started by C. Lurago, was completed in 1726 by the Prague architect F. M. Kaňka with the construction of the observatory tower and the eastern wing facing Marianské Square. F. M. Kaňka also built the remarkable Mirror Chapel, the library and the Mathematical Hall. All the architects who participated in the building of the Clementinum succeeded in achieving a unique complex which, however, represented a heavy mark on the small medieval organism of the Old Town.

The last Jesuit building to be erected in the Old Town was the Konvikt, an interesting, irregular structure which originated on the site of several houses by building round the large courtyard between Bartolomějská and Konviktská Streets. This building served as a secondary boarding school until the Jesuits order was abolished. Only later did it acquire a new function. The large hall of the former refectory became a place where artists of such resounding names as L. van Beethoven, A. Rubenstein and R. Wagner performed. The Konvikt was also the seat of an organ school, headed by the composer A. Dvořák.

Křižovnické Square also abounds in Baroque architecture. Throughout three centuries this relatively small area contained only the Gothic Old Town Bridge Tower, it being in the late 17th century that the noble Baroque building of the Church of St. Francis Seraphicus of the Knights of the Cross, illuminating Prague with its emerald green dome, originated. In the east the square was closed by the Jesuit Church of the Holy Saviour, gradually built by the two prominent architects C. Lurago and F. Caratti in the course or long years. When visiting this small square it is not possible to overlook the bronze Charles IV monument, set in place here in 1848 on the occasion of the five hundredth anniversary of the founding of Charles University, whose model was made by the Dresden sculptor E. J. Hähnel. Křižovnické Square, named after the Knights of the Cross, is a picturesque closed whole whose artistic values lie in the contrast of the Baroque with the Gothic.

Standing in the place where Husova and Karlova Streets intersect is Clam-Gallas Palace representing a rare sample of a Viennese palace building doing real credit to its brilliant creator, the Viennese court architect J. B. Fischer of Erlach. It stands in the place where the court of the brother of Charles IV, the Moravian margrave John Henry, was situated in the Middle Ages. Remainders of this court are preserved in the cellars of the palace. The exterior and interior decoration of Clam-Gallas Palace is remarkable. It is the work of the outstanding Baroque sculptor M. B. Braun.

In the early Eighties of the 18th century Prague entered the community of European cities with, apart from other things, the construction of independent theatre buildings. In the years 1781 to 1783 Count Nostic-Rieneck had a theatre built at his own cost on the area of the Fruit Market (Ovocný trh) in the Old Town in the spirit of the newly arriving Classical style. This building is memorable due to the fact that in 1787 Mozart's opera The Marriage of Figaro reaped great success here, followed on 29. October of the same year by the world premiere of the same composer's opera Don Giovanni. A conductor in the theatre was the German composer C. M. von Weber. In 1827 the first Czech opera, The Tinker (Dráteník) by F. Škroup, was performed here and the year 1834 was marked by the staging of J. K. Tyl's comedy Fidlovačka with music by F. Škroup. The song Where Is My Home (Kde domov můj), which later became the national anthem, was heard in it for the first time.

Standing in the neighbourhood of the Estates (Stavovské) Theatre, as in later years the Nostic Theatre began to be called after its owners, is the Carolinum, once a college of Charles University bestowed on the latter by King Václav IV. It was formerly the house of the royal Master of the Mint M. Rotlev which Václav IV had rebuilt so that it not only met college needs, but also so that it might become the centre of the university as a whole. Here there were flats and studies for the professors, lecture halls for the students and a rich library for everyone. The building also contained a steam bath and, for disturbers of the peace, a prison. The centre of the Carolinum was a large hall where academic degrees were awarded and where ceremonies and important assemblies of the whole university took place. This Gothic oriel, which is so typical of the Carolinum, was most likely a part of the old chapel of Rotlev's house.

The last extensive reconstruction of the Carolinum was carried out in the early 18th century and was the work of F. M. Kaňka. In 1930 Professor V. Birnbaum realized architectural, historical and archeological research of the whole building and in its course he discovered a great deal of the original building under Kaňka's alterations. Not until after World War II, however, was the Carolinum renewed after a project by J. Frágner. At that time the large hall along with the adjoining interiors was placed at the use of the university and it continues to serve its purpose. Its architectural design is interesting. J. Frágner symbolically divided it into a historical part, which had witnessed the historical events of the university and the whole nation, and a modern part intended for ceremonial occasions. Elements which had been discovered in the course of research were also incorporated in the renewed building. The most important of them is the Gothic portal, so perfectly preserved that for over six centuries it has continuously served its original purpose. The large hall, once the banquet hall of Rotlev's house, is decorated with a monumental gobelin created by M. Teinitzerová and a bronze figure of Charles IV, the work of K. Pokorný. The gobelin is a composition of decorative motifs from Charles's time, its centre part being based on the old university seal on which Charles IV is kneeling in front of St. Wenceslas.

When Václav I had walls built round the Old Town there was only a simple wall by the Vltava. Charles IV had its greater part demolished and for whole centuries the sandy bank of the river was lined with timber-yards, fishermen's cottages and rubbish-heaps. When floods occurred the water flowed into the streets of the Old Town even though a considerable deposit of earth from the past existed here. And so in the years 1841 to 1845 the Provincial Diet purchased all the yards, cottages, baths and mills stretching from New Avenue (Nové áleje), now called Národní Street, to the river and along it to Charles Bridge and had a high embankment wall built of hewn granite ashlars erected here. Thus there originated Prague's first embankment, named the Franz Embankment (Františkovo nábřeží) after the then ruling Austrian Emperor Franz. A chain bridge connecting Nové áleje with the street called Újezd in the Little Quarter (Malá Strana) was built at the same time as the embankment.

Until the end of the Sixties of the 19th century the square now named after Jan Palach was used for the dumping of rubbish. A large riding-school a timber store, an old compulsory study, a jail and an executioner's house stood here. In 1868 a chain footbridge was built in the direction from Kaprova Street to the bank of the Vltava in the Little Quarter and the year 1875 saw the beginning of the construction of an embankment wall here too. Opposite the footbridge a large area was defined for a future square, where the construction of monumental buildings was started in the early Eighties. The first to originate here in Neo-Renaissance style was the present Academy of Applied Art. The sunny northern side of the square was occupied by the building of the Rudolfinum, also built in Neo-Renaissance style. This attractive square was closed from the east by the building of the Philosophical Faculty of Charles University until the end of the Twenties of the 20th century.

334 The Chapel of the Holy Rood in Karolina Světlá Street is the oldest preserved Romanesque rotunda in Prague.

335 After its abolition **the former Jesuit** college was Prague's cultural centre. Concerts and balls were held in the refectory and one of Prague's first cinemas was opened here. In 1798 Beethoven gave a concert in the monastery hall and the first Czech ball took place here on 5 February.

336 Running from Bartolomějská Street to Konviktská Street is Průchodní Lane.

337 **Bethlehem Chapel** once housed the biggest lecture hall in medieval Prague. The reformer John Huss preached in it. In 1786 it was abolished and demolished. The restored chapel has its original ground-plan and onetime appearance. Its reconstruction was realized after old engravings and illustrations by J. Frágner from 1950 to 1953.

338 The House At the Halánek's (U Halánků) in Betlémské Square was first a renowned brewery and wine distillery. In the late 19th century it was owned by Vojta Náprstek, who founded a club, a lecture hall and a library with a reading-room and in 1862 a museum here. At first the museum was intended for the training of craftsmen and tradesmen, but later it became a general ethnographic one. Many exhibits came from Czech travellers. The core is formed by Náprstek's collection from his long stay in America.

339 The monastery Church of St. Anne was built in the early 14th century. The Templar order and later the Dominicans occupied the monastery. Joseph II abolished it and Jan Ferdinand of Schönfeld founded a printing house and the Imperial-Royal Postal Newspaper publishing house here in 1795. The Czech chronicler Václav Hájek of Libočany is buried in the church, now under reconstruction.

340

340 Aeriel view of the **Old Town,** strongly defined in the photo by the dark hatched line of Národní Street and Na Příkopě. The latter continues from the square Náměstí republiky through Revoluční Street to the Vltava. In the centre, above the aircraft wing, is the centre of the Old Town – Old Town Square. On its right the former Gall quarter dominated by St. Gall's Church.

341 **St. Gall's Church** was the parish church of Gall's Town. Charles IV had it rebuilt in High Gothic style and in the late 17th century it was Barocized. From 1627 it belonged to the Carmelites, who founded a monastery in it. Situated at the end of the southern side aisle is the tomb of the Baroque painter Karel Škréta.

342 The Dominican **Church of St. Giles** still has its fine Gothic form. Its interior was Barocized and decorated with frescos by Václav Vavřinec Reiner, whose tomb is situated in front of St. Vincent's altar.

343 **This house in Týnská Street** belonged to the wife of Václav Budovec of Budov, a Czech lord who was beheaded in Old Town Square in 1621

for his participation in the rebellion of the Czech Estates against the Hapsburgs. On the house is a memorial tablet and a bust of Budovec, the work of František Bílek.

344 Former Týn Court and the **Ungelt** customs house by it stood next to Prague's oldest market-place, on the intersecting point of trade routes, already in the 10th century. Every trade caravan had to halt here and pay duty (ungelt) into the prince's treasury.

345 **The Church of Our Lady of Týn** was built in the 14th century. It is sometimes called Týnský Church. This detail of the capital of one of its columns betrays that it was the most important church in Prague after St. Vitus's Cathedral at the Castle. It is an outstanding Gothic building whose tympanum on the northern portal is a brilliant work from the workshop of Peter Parler, Charles IV's chief builder. John Huss's predecessors – the German preacher Konrad Waldhauser and Tan Milíč of Kroměříž – preached in the church in the peried of the church reformation.

Situated near the high altar is the tombstone of the Danish astronomer Tychon Brahe. The painting Our Lady on the high altar (by K. Skréta), the Late Gothic Way of the Cross, the Gothic pulpit and the Late Gothic baldachin of the architect Matěj Rejsek are outstanding in the rich interior.

346   The Church of SS. Simon and Jude along with an old hospital stood on the bank of the Vltava in the place called Na Františku already in the 14th century. In 1620 the monastery was handed over to the order of Merciful Brethren, who opened a hospital here which until 1779 was Prague's only clinic. In 1847 it gained renown due to the monk F. C. Opitz anaesthetizing the first patient.

347   This house of red brick was built in 1910 by O. Novotný for **Štenc's Graphic Works.** Inspired by poetic Anglo-Saxon severity, it is nis most striking building in Prague.

348   Anežská Street leads to the convent whose oldest history is connected with the life of the royal daughter Anežka Přemyslovna. She gave up her high social position, founded in Prague a hospital and convent and became its first superior. The Church of the Holy Saviour of this convent was also the first burial place of the Přemyslids.

349   St. Castulus' Church was mentioned already in the founding charter of the Agnes Convent. It was built on a site belonging among the oldest parts of the Old Town.

350   The name of the romantic little street **Řásnovka** was changed with the times. In the 14th century it was called Slavičina and later Šnekova, Hlemýžd'ova, Slimákova and Plžova (the last four names mean „snail"). Mr. Šnek was the local manufacturer of playing cards. From 1940 to 1945 it was called Schneckengasse – Řásnovka.

350

351–352 An interesting thing with which very few cities can boast

The photo on the left shows a detail of A. Langweil's model portraying a part of the Old Town in a plastic manner. The aerial photo on the right shows approximately the same place.

Langweil was an employee of the university library and in his spare time he devoted his attention to the painting of miniature portraits and views. In 1826 a plastic model of Paris was exhibited in Prague and it inspired Langweil to create a similar model of Prague. He set to work with great enthusiasm and expended all his free time and financial means on achieving his aim. In the course of three years he produced model of the Old Town (about 600 houses), so that in July 1829 he was able to exhibit his work. In 1830 to 1831 he continued to work on the model. He supplemented the Old Town with church buildings and created the Jewish Town. In May 1831 he again presented his model to the public and then worked with the same passion and diligence on other parts of Prague. He created the Little Quarter and Hradčany. In 1824 he exhibited his model again, but after that year he did not continue in his work. The greatest obstruction was a lack of money. In his extreme distress he even requested the Emperor for help, but it arrived at the time when Langweil was ill and soon to die. As a record in the register of deaths of the priest's house belonging to the Church of St. Francis tells us he died of tuberculosis in the Eighties.

Visible by the lower edge of the photo of Langweil's model are the Old Town walls and seen in the centre is Old Town Square with the steeples of the Church of Our Lady of Týn and the towers of the Old Town Hall. The steeples of the Old Town church consecrated to S. Nicholas can be seen on the right of the Town Hall. In front of Týn Church are the steeples of St. James's Church. Spanning the Vltava in the background is Charles Bridge, Prague's only bridge at that time, with the conspicuous landmark on the right bank of the river – the Old Town Bridge Tower. By the upper edge of the photo is a part of the model of the Little Quarter.

In the aerial photo Old Town Square can be seen by the tip of the wing. One of Prague's oldest communications Celetná Street – runs along the draining edge of the wing. At this point the communication bends practically in a right angle (near the Powder Gate and the Municipal and House continues through the square Náměstí Republiky and Revoluční Street to the Vltava, thus demarcating the area of the former Old Town of Prague. The Old Town walls ran this way. In the middle of the photo is the Old Town and in the right-hand lower corner a part of the New Town, more precisely the Petrská quarter. Seen in the background are the Little Quarter and Hradčany and in the right-hand corner Letná Plain. Three of Prague's bridges are visible in the photo: Charles Bridge near the left side, Mánes Bridge in the centre and Čech Bridge below it. Between Čech and Mánes Bridges, on the Little Quarter bank of the river, is the building of the former Straka Academy, now the presidium of the government of the Czech Republic.

A. Langweil's plastic model of Prague is perhaps the most attractive exhibit in the Prague Museum in the Florenc quarter of Prague.

351

VII. THE NEW TOWN (NOVÉ MĚSTO)

The imperial charter issued by Charles IV was the culmination of his aim to found the New Town of Prague, because the Old Town no longer sufficed to hold all the population. The sovereign had the construction of the New Town started shortly after the completion of the building of the Royal Palace at the Castle.

Four important wholes can still be distinguished in the ground-plan of the New Town: the central part, whose backbone was the Horse Market, now Wenceslas Square, the southern part with the Cattle Market as its centre, now Charles Square, the north-eastern part by the Mountain Gate, which was the Hay Market, now Senovážné Square, and the southern slope which Charles IV had planted with parks and vineyards. Before the New Town was founded Charles IV laid the foundations of two important church buildings. The first was the Church of Our Lady of the Snows and the second the Emmaus „Na Slovanech" church and monastery. Other sacral buildings were the Church of St. Charles the Great „Na Karlově", St. Henry's Church, St. Stephen's Church, St. Catherine's Church, the Church of Our Lady „Na Slupi" and St. Apollinarius's Church. All these buildings have remained preserved and although some of them were subjected to modifications during the centuries they still manifest their Gothic origin. As regards secular buildings, the construction of the New Town Hall was started during Charles IV's lifetime. Charles Square (the Cattle Market) was the chief market-place in the New Town where, in addition to cattle, many different products were sold.

The main link between the Old and the New Town was the Horse Market, to which most of the streets ran. Horses were sold in its upper part and the goods of various craftsmen, who newly settled in the New Town, were sold on stands.

The culmination of Charles's building activity was stone Charles Bridge, an outstanding technical work supervised by P. Parler. On 7 April, 1348 Charles IV founded a university in Prague, the first institution of its kind north of the Alps.

With its 40,000 inhabitants Prague became a big city during the reign of Charles IV.

The appearance of the New Town remained unchanged in essence for two centuries, a new style penetrating into it only after the defeat of the Czech Estates in the Battle on the White Mountain (1620).

The Baroque was first limited only to church and noble buildings – more in the Little Quarter and the Old Town than in the New Town. The Italian architect C. Lurago along with M. Reiner designed St. Ignatius' Church on the corner of Charles Square and Ječná Street and a Franciscan church originated opposite the Powder Gate after plans by D. Orsi.

Prague's Baroque architecture culminated with the work of K. I. Dienzenhofer, who, with his father Christopher, built the Church of St. Charles Borromaeus, followed by a whole number of churches, mostly in the Little Quarter and the Old Town. St. John on the Rock in Vyšehradská Street is an exception. Late Baroque construction was concentrated in the New Town boulevards Staré áleje (Old Avenues – now Příkopy) and Nové áleje (New Avenues – now Národní Street). The older parts of these streets were planted with lime avenues and the newer parts with chestnut trees. The new function of the two streets necessitated their lining with ostentatious buildings and so three Baroque palaces originated on the New Town side of Old Avenues in the mid-18th century, Schirding Palace and the large Ursuline convent, designed by Marco Antonio Canavel, being built in New Avenues. Preserved in its original form since that time is also Sylva Taroucca Palace, built from 1743 to 1751 by K. I. Dienzenhofer and A. Lurago in Příkopy, and the palace of the Porges of Portheim and Kaňka's house in Národní Street.

The Baroque also marked Prague's fortifications. The medieval walls from Charles' time did not suffice, as proved during the Thirty Years War, to secure the defence of the towns of Prague and so directly after the war the Emperor ordered a new defence system to be projected. The zone of new walls, situated in front of the old Gothic ones, was strengthened with forty huge bastions and access to Prague was gained through eleven gates. Thus Prague was enclosed by a huge fortification system in whose construction C. Lurago also participated in the New Town.

There were four gates in the New Town walls. Poříčská (Poříč) in Karlín, Nová (New) in the Hay Market, Koňská (Horse) in the Horse Market and Sviňská (Sow) or also St. Paul's in the place where Sokolská Street joins Žitná Street. The walls stretched from the Vltava to Karlov in a curve, meeting up there with the Vyšehrad fortifications.

In the early 19th century the then Prague burgrave Count Karel Chotek had park roads built and Chotek's Promenades soon became the frequent destination of walks. True, the lost war against Prussia in 1866 proved the lack of purposefulness of the walls in modern military strategy, but the State did not hasten to secure their demolition. Not until 1874 was this started, making the New Town open to the surrounding communities. However, before this unusual building activity was realized in the New Town, affecting all three main squares and the streets leading to them. The Late Baroque made way for a new style which at Napoleon's time spread through Europe. The striking buildings of the Classical period include in the New Town the palace U Hybernů (At the Iberians), the Church of the Holy Rood in Příkopy and the building of Masaryk Station. In the later half of the 19th century buildings influenced by romantic historism originated in the New Town.

Architects J. Zítek and J. Schulz built the National Theatre in Czech Renaissance style and the latter built the monumental National Museum on the site of the former Horse Gate.

The basic principles of the Czech Renaissance formed by the Art Nouveau were manifested in the building of the Provincial Bank in Příkopy, built after plans by O. Polívka. The epoch of pseudo-historical styles ended in the mid-nineties. A prominent representative of the transition from historism to the Art Nouveau was B. Ohman, who began with the Neo-Baroque buildings of the former Valter Palace in Voršilská Street and the building of the present Office for Patents and Inventions on the corner of Jindřišská Street and Wenceslas Square and progressed to the Art Nouveau building of the Central Hotel in Hybernská Street, built by Q. Bělský. The most ostentatious Art Nouveau building is the Evropa Hotel (formerly Šroubek) in Wenceslas Square. It was designed by A. Dryák and B. Bedelmayer. The Art Nouveau influenced other architects as well. For example, O. Polívka designed the large building of the U Nováků (At the Novaks) department store in Vodičkova Street from 1902 to 1903 and J. Fanta projected the Main Station built from 1901 to 1909. At the end of the first decade of the new century the Art Nouveau changed into the style of the individualistic moderns. It was in this spirit that J. Kotěra designed a house in Jungmannova Street for the music publisher M. Urbánek and the Mozart Concert Hall. The old navigation commmunity of Podskalí disappeared in connection with the regulation of the Vltava and the clearance of its banks, a number of remarkable buildings originating on its site. These include the building of the General Pensions Institute, the work of J. Kotěra and I. Zasche.

J. Zasche and his friend P. Janák designed the palace for the Italian Riunine Adriatica Insurance Office in Národní Street, decorated by leading sculptors of the time: J. Štursa, O. Guttfreund, K. Dvořák and B. Kafka.

353 The Old Town, the Little Quarter, Hradčany and the New Town formed the **four towns of Prague** until 1784. The aerial photo shows practically all the Old Town. In the foreground is a part of the New Town and in the background, behind the Vltava, the Little Quarter and Hradčany.

354 B. Smetana established a music school and composed his operas The Bartered Bride and Dalibor in Lažanský Palace.

355 The contrast formed by the historic buildings in Národní Street and the New Stage Theatre.

356 **Dunaj Palace** with a travertine façade is the work of the architects O. Polívka and A. Foehr of 1930.

357 On 17. 11. 1989 the arcade of Baroque Kaňka's House witnessed a rough police attack on the quiet demonstration of students which ignited the anti-communist revolution in Czechoslovakia.

358 In the late 18th century **Platýz** in Národní Street was owned by Baron Jakub Wimmer, the founder of Prague's parks and vineyards.

359 **Adrie Palace** was inspired by Italian Early Renaissance architecture. It was built by P. Janák and J. Zasche in 1925. Its façade was decorated by leading sculptors of the time.

360 The former **ARA department store** had one of the first steel bearing structures in Prague.

361 The Art Nouveau portal in Jungmannova Square.

362 View of Jungmannovo Square when coming out of Národní třída Station of the Metro.

354

363 Aerial view of the **centre of the New Town.** Its main axes Wenceslas Square, Jindřišská Street, Vodičkova Street, Příkopy and the whole street network have remained unchanged since the town originated. It cannot be excluded that the New Town was projected by the French architect Matthias of Arras, one of the builders of St. Vitus's Cathedral.

364 The idea of crowning the former building of the one-time stock exchange with a new two-storeyed superstructure came from architect K. Prager. It originated after World War II, when the building was adapted for the needs of the National Assembly.

365 J. V. Myslbek combined the **St. Wenceslas monument** in Wenceslas Square with sculptures of other Czech patron saints – S. Ludmilla, St. Procopius, St. Adalbert and St. Ivan. St. Ivan was later replaced with the Blessed Agnes (now St. Agnes).

366 One of the last Baroque buildings in Wenceslas Square is **the Adrie Hotel.** It remembers the time when the square was a horse market.

367 **The Grand Hotel Evropa,** formerly Šroubek, is an Art Nouveau work of F. Ohmann, who came to Prague after studying at the Technical University in Vienna and designed a number of buildings here.

368 **Wenceslas Square** was one of the three centres of the New Town founded by Charles IV in 1348. Its axis from the north-west to the south-east fully corresponds to contemporary urban requirements.

369 **Koruna Palace** on the corner of Wenceslas Square and Příkopy is the work of the architect A. Pfeiffer, who studied at the School of Applied Art in Prague under J. Kotěra, from whom he adopted the modernistic conception of architecture combining constructiveness with decorativeness. This style is especially manifested in Koruna Palace, decorated with sculptures by V. Sucharda. This building, on whose ground-floor the first Prague bistro was opened in the early 20th century, has a tower-shaped corner terminated with a crown.

364

367

365

368

366

369

370 **Sylva-Taroucca Palace** in Příkopy is a Rococo building which originated after projects by K. I. Dienzenhofer and A. Lurago. The sculptured decoration of the façade and the interior staircase is the work of I. Platzer. Gothic cellars have been preserved in the building. An Ethnographical Museum was installed here from 1895 to 1905.

371 According to a legend the street **Nekázanka** is connected with the history of the building-up of the New Town of Prague. Its founder Charles IV strictly followed the urban plans in which he himself had participated. Once when on a journey of inspection through Prague he discovered a street whose building he had not ordered and allegedly said that it was to be called Nekázanka (Unordered) for all time. Roofed bridges connected the two bank palaces constructed in Czech Renaissance style after designs by O. Polívka.

372 The huge, granite-faced **palace of the Czech National Bank** was built from 1936 to 1938 by the architect F. Roith on the site of a pseudo-historic building from whose gable a bronze statue of a genius with a lion, the work of the sculptor A. Popp, was transferred to the top of the new palace.

373 Present Hybernská Street was once called Horská after Horská Gate at its end from where people travelled to Kutná Hora. Charles IV had St. Ambrosius' Monastery built at its beginning. After the Battle on the White Mountain it fell into the hands of the Franciscan Iberians. The huge building, whose façade faces the crossroads by the Powder Gate, serves as an exhibition palace. It originated as the result of the reconstruction of the Baroque Church of Our Lady, which in later years was converted into a customs house. It was designed by the architect J. Fischer, who took the remote building of the old mint in Berlin as his model. Standing at the entrance to the building are two robust Doric columns and on the second floor there can be seen a typical Classical hemispherical window. The wide façade terminates with a cornice with a tympanum which is decorated with a relief of the Austrian imperial eagle.

374 The site of the Municipal House of Prague was once occupied by the King's Court, built by Václav IV. All his successors lived in it, until Vladislav Jagiello who finally moved to Prague Castle. The court enjoyed its greatest period of glory at the time of George of Poděbrady. In those days there was a busy centre here where deputations and diplomats gathered and where assemblies and provincial Diets took place. It was from here that the idea of inviting European countries to peaceful cooperation came already in the 15th century. **The Municipal House** is the best-known Art Nouveau building in Prague. It was designed by A. Balšánek and O. Polívka who won a public competition with their ingenious symmetrical design based on the principle of a diagonal rhomboidal building site. Apart from the big Smetana Concert Hall there are numerous richly decorated social rooms in the building.

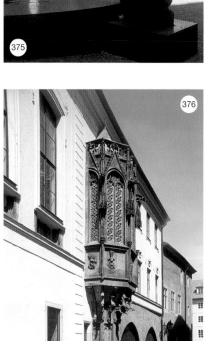

and it is the central university building. Among other things a beautiful Gothic oriel has remained of Rotlev's original house.

377 Situated in the very centre of Prague, in the close vicinity of Wenceslas Square, is the green oasis of the Franciscan Gardens. There was once a cemetery with a gate decorated with a Gothic tympanum in a part of it. This valuable work of 1346 portraying the coronation of the virgin Mary, Charles IV and his first consort Blanche of Valois was heavily damaged, thus being replaced with a copy.

In the background of the photo is the Church of Our Lady of the Snows, founded in 1379 by Charles IV. However, only the torso of this church building, the biggest in Prague, has been preserved. Only the presbytery was built, the Hussite wars bringing construction work to an end. The church was the place of assembly of the Hussites and at the beginning of the wars it was the centre of the Hussite radical wing, headed ideologically by the preacher Jan Želivský. The building of the monastery has a Renaissance character. The priest's house with a huge Baroque portal dates in 1788.

378 **The house At the Two Golden Bears** (U dvou zlatých medvědů) is interesting due to the fact that at the end of the 19th century the German journalist and writer E. E. Kisch of Prague, author of many works devoted especially to the life or the riff-raff and the underworld of Prague, spent his childhood in it.

375 On 7. 4. 1348 King Charles IV founded a university with four faculties (devoted to law, theology, medicine and art – philosophy) in Prague. After World War II the university buildings were renewed after a project by J. Frágner. The photo shows the modernized façade facing Ovocný trh (Fruit Market).

376 The house of the former royal master of the mint Jan Rotlev on the corner of Železná Street and Ovocný trh was one of the first seats of the newly founded colleges of Charles University. It is called the **Carolinum**

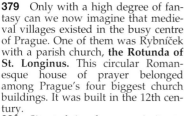

379 Only with a high degree of fantasy can we now imagine that medieval villages existed in the busy centre of Prague. One of them was Rybníček with a parish church, **the Rotunda of St. Longinus.** This circular Romanesque house of prayer belonged among Prague's four biggest church buildings. It was built in the 12th century.

380 Situated in close proximity to the Rotunda of St. Longinus is **St. Stephen's Church,** founded by Charles IV immediately after the New Town of Prague.

Charles's Prague churches are a real delight for lovers of the building art. As a passionate collector he had the size, form and architecture of the individual buildings in which he was an ideological participant designed in different ways, so that they represent a real sample-book of Gothic church architecture.

381 **St. Catherine's Church,** likewise built by Charles IV, is square with a single column in its centre. The Emperor had it built for the Augustians. Preserved of the original building is the remarkable Gothic square steeple passing into an octagon. The other parts of the church were built later.

382 **Michna's Summer Palace,** which was later called Amerika, was the first building erected in Prague by the young K. I. Dienzenhofer.

383 **The Church „Na Karlově"** is said to have been built on the wish of Charles IV by the young builder as his first church building. He was given the task of erecting a bold vault with eight rays which was meant to bring

the octagonal burial chapel of Charles the Great at Aachen to mind. When they completed the church no one wanted to demolish the scaffolding. Everyone was afraid that the vault would collapse and so they burnt the scaffolding. The vault did not collapse, but the young builder was fished out from the Vltava. He had run away from the fire and jumped into the river, not believing in the success of his work. Only the peripheral masonry of the original Gothic building has been preserved. The vault of the presbytery dates in 1498 and the vault of the nave to which the old legend is attached is as late as the year 1575. The architecture, interior decorations and furnishings of the church are Baroque and are the work of F. M. Kaňka. A part of the New Town fortifications can be seen below the church. The walls visible in the photo are newer, but they stand on the site of those whose foundation stone was laid by Charles IV himself in 1348. They were built round the whole of the New Town in the unbelievably short period of two years.

Its general urban conception makes it clear that Charles IV wanted to make Prague an enormous fortress protected by the Castle in the north and by Vyšehrad in the south. For this reason he also widened the Hradčany walls and the Hunger Wall and incorporated the Little Quarter walls and Vyšehrad fortress into a single fortress system. Thus there originated a work which had no like in Europe in the 15th century.

384 The Cattle Market, now Charles Square (Karlovo náměstí) was the biggest area in the New Town of Prague – Forum magnum. Standing in its centre, on the corner with Ječná Street, is **the Church of St. Ignatius of Loyola**, founder of the Jesuit order. Its façade is noteworthy for the statue of St. Ignatius framed with gold rays. The interior of the church is typically Baroque – a large hall with side chapels and tribunes. The vault and walls are remarkable for their rich stucco decoration supplemented with the figures of Jesuit saints and Czech patrons.

In the park there is a number of sculptures, among others a **statue of Eliška Krásnohorská,** who portrayed the appearance of the Cattle Market in her novel Zvonečková královna (The Harebell Queen).

385 The only monument of the oldest times in Charles Square is **the New Town Hall.** It was built from 1377, but it began to change conspicuously in the early 16th century. It gained a Renaissance form and only its cellars and the column hall have remained from the Gothic period. The tower still has the form in which it was built-on on to the Town Hall in the 15th century.

Similarly as in every Town Hall, there was also a prison here. It was so strong that for a time it was called the Prague Bastille.

On 30 June, 1419 the raging Hussites threw two counsellors from the windows. This event, which historians began to call the first Prague defenestration, ignited the Hussite wars.

386 **Salm House** on the corner of Řeznická Street and Charles Square belonged to the Baroque sculptor M. B. Braun in the first half of the 18th century. He died in it in 1738. The house was originally Renaissance, its portal having been preserved from that time. Later it was barocized.

387 Standing in Resslova Street is **the Church of St. Charles Borromaeus,** built next to the house of the emeritus priests. This Baroque building of K. I. Dienzenhofer was restored in 1934 for the needs of the orthodox church and consecrated to the missionaries SS. Cyril and Method. On a wall of the church there is a bronze memorial tablet by F. Bělský recalling that the parachutists who assassinated Reinhard Heydrich, the imperial protector in Bohemia and Moravia and SS general, in May 1942, during the Nazi occupation of Czechoslovakia, took refuge in the crypt and fought their last battle against the Nazis there.

388 **Faust's House** is the subject of a legend which informs us that the intrigues of Johannes Faust and the devil took place here. However, no Dr. Faust lived in the Baroque core of the Renaissance house in the southern part of Charles Square, but in the 14th century it was the scene of alchemy experiments carried out by certain Prince Opavský and during the reign of Rudolph II by the English alchemist E. Kelley.

389 **The Church of St. John on the Rock** is an outstanding work of K. I. Dienzenhofer. In its western façade there is a remarkable couple of towers built slantingly towards each other. Inside there is a fresco The Celebration of St. John Nepomuk by K. Kovář and on the high altar there is a wooden sculpture of St. John which was carved by J. Brokoff as a model for the statue on Charles Bridge.

390 **The Church of Our Lady** was also built by K. I. Dienzenhofer. In the wing connecting the church with the monastery there is a Late Gothic panel painting of the Madonna of the 15th century.

391 **The Church of Our Lady „Na Slupi"** was built at the same time as the monastery of the Servites. It is a Gothic building with a characteristic slender steeple in its façade.

392 **The Church of the Holiest Trinity** in Trojická Street was once the parish church of Podskalí, an ancient and characteristic community of raftsmen, sandmen, fishermen, timbermen and icemen.

393 **Podskalí** is brought to mind by the statue of a raftsman on the house on the corner of Podskalská and Ladova Streets. The house is memorable due to the fact that the first illustrator of The Good Soldier Švejk lived in it from 1925 to 1957.

The „Na Slovanech" Monastery, also called Emmaus, belonged to Podskalí. It was founded by Charles IV and until the Hussite wars it was the biggest centre of culture and art in Prague. It was heavily damaged during the air raid on Prague on 14. 2. 1945 and after the war it was reconstructed. Architect F. M. Černý set a concrete roof recalling the sails of a ship on the roof of the monastery church. It creates an exceptionally modern impression, but at the same time it brines the original Gothic appearance of the church to mind due to its height and conception.

394 **„Na Výtoni"** was once a customs house where salt imported from the Austrian Salt Chamber along the Vltava was taxed similarly as timber transported on rafts to Podskali. The „Na Výtoni" customs house is a Late Gothic building with a frame upper floor built about 1500. The fine portal with the emblem of the New Town dates in 1671, when the building was purchased by the community of the New Town. Interesting material and documentary relics concerning the past of Podskalí are housed in its interior. Practically nothing of Podskalí has remained. Its end came about suddenly at the turn of the 19th and 20th centuries due to the regulation of the Vltava and the clearance of its banks.

IX. VYŠEHRAD

Vyšehrad is another equally important landmark of Prague which, like the Castle, is also clearly visible from the banks of the River Vltava. It has a similarly long and interesting history, but not so many treasures and art and architecturaly monuments have been preserved on Vyšehrad. Nevertheless, a walk through this place is not only very interesting, but also pleasant. When gazing at the remainders and foundations of old buildings we become aware of the destiny of Vyšehrad, which was always connected with Prague and the Czech principality and kingdom. In its present form Vyšehrad is actually a large park spreading out behind the gates of the Baroque fortification system and high ramparts rising above the Vltava on its left bank. There is a small, almost intimate museum here and it is possible to visit the casemates in the underground part of the fortress. Lawns and big trees surround the freely situated church buildings. The Neo-Romantic Church of SS. Peter and Paul has been beautifully restored. Prominent personages and artists lie at rest in the national cemetery. And from the whole periphery of the walls an entirely unusual view of Prague can be obtained in all directions. Vyšehrad is connected with ancient legends and myths, with the origin of the Přemyslid family of princes and later kings and with the legendarv Princess Libuše, who prophesied the future of Prague from me high rock overlooking the Vltava: I see a great city whose glory touches the stars. Our first chronicler and European intellectual Cosmas (d. 1125), deacon of the St. Vitus chapter in Prague, placed this statement in the princess' mouth in Latin: Urbem conspicio fama quae sidera tangent. In Cosmas's chronicle we can also find the first written mention of Vyšehrad in connection with the year 1003. Vyšehrad is about one hundred years younger than Prague Castle.

For Vyšehrad the origin of a Slavonic settlement meant the building of a castle site in the first half of the 10th century. At the end of the same century a pre-Romanesque sacral building was founded here with a cross ground-plan. The pre-Slavonic settlement is much older and its culture is named after archeological finds.

During the reigns of Prince Boleslav II and Boleslav III (967–1003) there was a mint on Vyšehrad where silver Přemyslid denars were coined. Some of the thirty-two types of these coins can be seen in the previously mentioned museum.

Prince Vratislav II (1061–1092) raised the castle site to a seat of princes. From 1085 Vratislav was the first Czech king, but this title was not yet hereditary. The Vyšehrad chapter, which was independent of the Prague bishopric and directly subordinated to the Pope, was founded (1070). A church consecrated to SS. Peter and Paul, a rotunda, a basilica and new stone fortifications were built and the residential palace was separated from the church buildings by a bridge, whose masonry has been partly preserved to the present. The Přemyslid princes ruled over Prague and the country from Vyšehrad until 1140.

The Emperor and Czech king Charles IV (1316–1378) renewed the glory of Vyšehrad. New fortifications connected the walls with the New Town of Prague. The chapter church was rebuilt after the model of basilicas of southern France and with its length of 110 metres it surpassed all Prague's churches of that time. We can imagine the growth of Vyšehrad and the surrounding vineyards also according to the fact that in 1361 a stone water mains was built which carried water from as far away as Pankrác. However, of the greatest importance was the new tradition which originated during coronations. Charles IV decreed that every new Czech king had to go on foot to Vyšehrad, look at shoes made of bast and hang an equally simple bag on his shoulder in order to remind him that Czech rulers came from the people. In order to strengthen Czech statemindedness Charles IV topicalized the legend about Libuše: When they reproached the princess with the words: Woe to men ruled over by a woman, a clairvoyant urge made her send for Přemysl the Ploughman. He left his work in the fields and, as the founder of the ruling Přemyslid family, devoted himself to the duties of a prince.

It was here that, during the Hussite wars, Hussite troops defeated the Crusaders of King Sigismund and plundered Vyšehrad in 1420. The attempt made by George of Poděbrady to renew Vyšehrad after 1450 was not successful, although plots of land could be gained here free of charge. The community never had more than several dozen houses. At the end of the Thirty Years War (1648) the Swedes damaged the walls and from 1653 a Baroque fortress was built. Upper Vyšehrad ceased to exist as a township and below the walls Vyšehrad developed as an independent settlement administratively connected to Prague in 1884 as the sixth town quarter. However, it had its own Town Hall already from 1765.

In the 19th century and especially during its later half Czech patriots and the romantic intelligentsia showed ever greater interest in Vyšehrad, which strengthened the self-assurance of the Czech nation, which had undergone a language and cultural revival. In the renewed and well-laid-out cemetery round the Church of SS. Peter and Paul it gained a dienified monument to its modern cultural representatives. The first to be buried here in accordance with this idea was V. Hanka, the discoverer of ancient manuscripts which were supposed to indicate the oldest beginnings of Czech literature. After long disputes it was ascertained that they were fakes produced by Hanka himself. Later Slavín (Pantheon) was built on the eastern side of the cemetery (1889–1893). The summit of A. Wiehl's architecture is decorated with a winged statue „The Genia of the Country" by A. Maudr. In actual fact the structure is a kind of solemn common grave. The first to be buried here was the writer Julius Zeyer (1902), who apart from other works, wrote the narrative poem Vyšehrad. Bedřich Smetana (1824–1884) opened his well-known cycle Má vlast (My Country) with a symphonic poem called Vyšehrad and in his opera Libuše, whose plot is set on legendary Vyšehrad, he revived the Přemyslid myth. Bedřich Smetana has a simple gravestone among the other graves. The inhabitants of Prague commonly use the name Slavín for the whole of the renowned cemetery on Vyšehrad, however.

To date six hundred personalities of Czech culture and science have been buried in Vyšehrad cemetery. It has become a kind of place of pilgrimage and the graves of classics and more recently interred artists are decorated with fresh flowers especially on their anniversaries. To be seen here is in fact a special gallery or sculptures, because the tombstones are the work of the best Czech sculptors; the romantic J. V. Myslbek, the symbolist and Art Nouveau sculptor F. Bílek and the moderns K. Lidický, J. Wagner and B. Benda.

Vyšehrad is emblazoned not only with a Czech myth, but also with many other legends. Libuše's treasure is supposed to be hidden in the rock, soldiers from ancient wars wander along the walls and seek their stories and the devil himself, with whom a certain Vyšehrad priest got mixed up, also has a place of his own here. St. Peter advised the priest how to trick the devil. Before the priest finished his sermon, the devil had to bring a big stone column from the Church of Our Lady in Rome to Vyšehrad. The devil was naturally unable to fulfil this task in time and in his anger he threw the column into the church through its roof, whereupon it broke into three pieces. When this story was told to rational Joseph II, who visited Vyšehrad, the Emperor said that the devil's three pieces of stone were to be removed from the church. And so since 1888 they have attracted the attention of visitors among the trees behind the cemetery.

Since 1962 Vyšehrad has been a National Cultural Monument and since 1966 systematic archeological research has been continuosly carried out here.

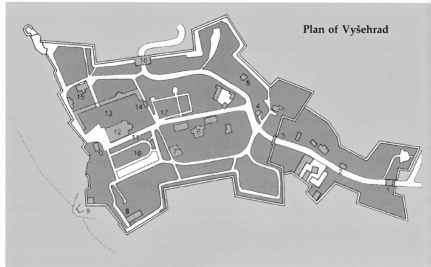

Plan of Vyšehrad

Legends to plan

The contour of the plan indicates the brick walls of the Baroque citadel which originated in the mid-17th century. Its Baroque form with corner bastions has been preserved to the present.

1 Tábor Gate (Táborská brána)
2 Gate called Špička
3 Leopold Gate (Leopoldova brána)
4 St. Martin's Rotunda
5 Chapel of Our Lady in the Wall
6 New Deanery (exposition of the history of Vyšehrad)
7 St. Lawrence's Basilica
8 Former burgrave's house of the time of Charles IV
9 Gotic ruin called Libuše's Bath
10 Czech Mythology – monumental statues by J. V. Myslbek
11 Remainders of a Romanesque bridge
12 Church of SS. Peter and Paul
13 Vyšehrad Cemetery
14 Pantheon (Slavín) in Cemetery
15 New Provost's House
16 Brick (Cihelná) or Chotek Gate
17 Devil's Column

395 The traditional church emblem of the Vyšehrad chapter, which on the basis of a confirmation of King Vratislav II of 1088 had a provost, a deacon and 12 canons.

396 In the later half of the 17th century the seat of princes, kings and the church was fortified with brick walls. Since 1655 access to the fortress from the east has been gained from Pankrác through **Tábor Gate.**

397 However, the main rampart of the fortress is closed or opened with

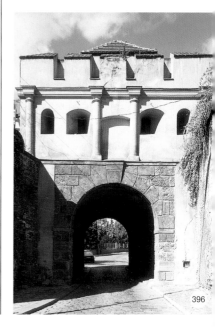

Leopold Gate (1678), designed by C. Lurago and richly decorated by the sculptor G. B. Álliprandi. Whether we set out from here to the right or upwards to the left we follow the periphery of the wall with a view of the whole of Prague.

398 In 1420, after the defeat of King Sigismund's troops, the Hussites plundered Vyšehrad, this being regretted also by the patriots, since they preferred the Utraquists to the Crusaders. It is up to archeologists to discover traces of the former glory of Vyšehrad. However, St. Martin's Rotunda of the later half of the 11th century has survived the ages. It is the oldest rotunda in Prague. From time to time divine services take place in the building.

399 Let it be recalled that the patrons of the Czech Land are St. Wenceslas, St. Ludmila, St. Adalbert and St. Procopius. Their mosaic portraits (1882) decorate the plague column (1714) of the nearby rotunda.

400 Standing behind the plague column built into the fortification rampart is a miniature chapel (1748) consecrated to Our Lady in the Walls. In 1882 it was subjected to Neo-Renaissance alterations carried out by B. Münzberger and A. Baum.

SV VOJTĚCH
Z PRVNÍ POLOVINY
18. STOLETÍ

401 Vyšehrad experienced an illustrious period during the reign of Charles IV. In the course of two years only – 1348 to 1350 – a new fortification was built and the way to Prague from the south had to run through Vyšehrad, guarded in southerly direction by the magnificent **gate called Špička.** We know it only from written records and later engravings as a small castle serving defence purposes. Only its Gothic masonry and the torsos of arches have been preserved.

402 In 1913 Professor R. Jedlička founded an institute for physically afflicted youth. **The oldest building of Jedlička's Institute** lies between Tábor and Leopold Gates.

403 The interior of the building of **the New Deanery** (J. Niklas, 1879) acquaints the visitor with the history of Vyšehrad.

404 A Baroque statue of St. Adalbert.

405 Until 1879 the more modest, but older **equestrian statue of St. Wenceslas** Q. J. Bendl, 1678) stood in the centre of Wenceslas Square.

406 In this romantic park in front of the New Provost's House there is also **a statue of the provost Štulc** (Š. Zálešák, 1910).

407 If we walk through Vyšehrad Cemetery from the Church of SS. Peter and Paul in the direction „towards Prague" i. e., in northerly direction, we come across a suprise in the form of the Neo-Romantic building of **the New Provost's House** (J. Niklas, 1872) standing in the middle of the Park.

176

408

409

410

408 The Devil's Columns leaning against each other in the park behind the eastern wall of the cemetery. As a whole the column may have supported a Romanesque basilica, whose shadow perhaps imdicated the arrival of the solstice to the ancient Slavs.

409 Remainders of a stone Romanesque bridge of the first half of the 12th century have been discovered below the present ground level. It was a part of the fortifications of the palace or the seat of the Přemyslids.

410 The western façade of the Church of SS. Peter and Paul in its Neo-Gothic form (J. Mocker and later F. Mikš). The original basilica was reconstructed and enlarged in the Gothic, Renaissance and Baroque styles (1723–1729). The entrance portal is decorated with sculptures by S. Zálešák (1901) which portray The Last Judgement. Přemyslid princes are Buried in the crypt. Outstanding among the Neo-Gothic decorations is the panel painting Our Lady of the Rains (c. 1350).

411 The original **foundations of the Royal Palace,** 11th – 12th century.

412 Přemysl the Ploughman and Princess Libuše as the sculptor J. V. Myslbek imagined the founders of the Přemyslid dynasty.

413 View from the western edge of the walls towards the north. In the foreground the remainder of a 14th century tower, which is now in the exhibition hall. On the rocky promontory the ruins of „Libuše's bath".

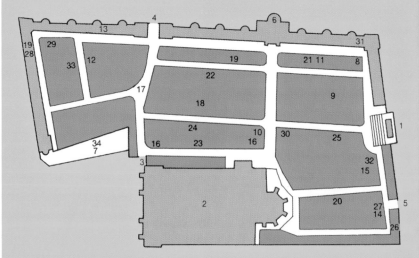

Plan of the Cemetery on Vyšehrad

A survey of important graves can be found by the entrance to the cemetery, or in the special guides which are available on Vyšehrad. We are presenting some ot them for the sake of orientation: first under the number on our plan and then the number of the given grave in the national cemetery.

414 Arcades with graves line the northern side of the cemetery. The Neo-Renaissance open galleries have vaults and in the middle part there is a small chapel which also served as a mortuary and its lower part as a crypt for certain members of the Vyšehrad chapter.

415 The grave of the writer Karel Čapek (1890–1938). Situated on the top of the grave column symbolizing a rustic chapel is the emblem of the former Czechoslovak Republic. The monument was designed by Karel Ča-

414

pek's brother Josef, whose name is symbolically brought to mind in the cemetery by an inscription – Grave far away – because he died in a Nazi concentration camp in 1945.

416 The Vyšehrad Pantheon dominates the eastern side of the cemetery. It is the common vault of the most prominent personalities of Czech culture.

417 The grave of the well-known actor Vlastimil Fišar (1926–1991) was decorated with a statue by the leading contemporary sculptor O. Zoubek.

418 The tombstone of Antonín

Dvořák (1841–1904). The world-renowned composer and representative of Czech romantic music and his wife Anna rest in peace here. We wish to remind visitors that apart from famous personalities former artists whose names are now forgotten in our cultural history are also buried in this cemetery. Their graves are covered with green vegetation. And the rows of simple graves of nuns of the Elizabethan order situated by the southern side of the nearby entrance to the church impress and move us with their modest piety.

X. SMÍCHOV

The Smíchov brewery (1871) brews more than one million hectolitres of beer of the „Old Spring" (Staropramen) brand every year. This is not the only important feature of Smíchov, however. Smíchov is the core of one of the biggest districts of Prague with over 100,000 inhabitants. Some 80,000 people live on the housing estates of the South West Town. This district originated as the result of the merging of 20 villages and communities and the B line of the Metro runs from Anděl Station to Zličín on the very edge of Prague.

Traffic crossroads, commerce, services, industry, especially the engineering industry developing here since the 19th century, the modernization of ostentatious blocks of town buildings from the periods of Romantism and the Art Nouveau and housing estates for the working-class, a paradise for entrepreneurs and town-planners, but also for the visitor who is not interested in making money, but in spending it and enjoying a new experience – all these necessitate a warning: take care not to become a prisoner of the grey streets. This applies in the case of all the districts of Prague with the exception of the centre of the city. The Old Town, the New Town, the Little Quarter and Hradčany offer something interesting at every step. Apart from the centre of the city, the visitor must not proceed step by step, but jump from one oasis to another. To put it briefly, he must know what he wants to see and where to find and enjoy it. We are illustrating this kind and practical recommendation by means of a visit to Smíchov.

Smíchov spreads out on the left bank of the River Vltava between the Railway Bridge in the south and Legion Bridge, which runs into the street Národní třída. Paradoxically, it is possible to orientate oneself easily on the right bank of the river. Everyone knows where Vyšehrad is situated. It is characterized by the twin steeples of the Church of SS. Peter and Paul on a huge rock overlooking the Vltava. And everyone knows where the National Theatre is situated. It is between these two points that Smíchov lies – but on the left bank!

The quickest and the easiest way to reach Smíchov is by the Metro. You must use the B line and get out at Anděl Station. Somewhat more exacting, but also more interesting are the three other most suitable possibilities.

Let us now cross one of the bridges. From Vyšehrad over the Railway Bridge (Železniční most). Footpaths for pedestrians run along the railway lines on this arched iron structure (1901). Steamboats are anchored by the banks of the river. The Vltava is nearly 300 metres wide at this spot. The embankments are lined with Romantic and Art Nouveau buildings. Visible in the distance is the panorama of Hradčany, which we can also admire from the three other bridges running, as we say, „from Prague" to Smíchov. From the Monastery „Na Slovanech" let us make our way across Palacký Bridge (Palackého most), built in 1878. Before crossing Jirásek Bridge (Jiráskův most), built in 1933, we should take note of the ancient towers and mills and waterworks by the bank. And should we wish to reach Smíchov by crossing Legion Bridge (most Legií) from the National Theatre we can descend some steps leading to Marksmen's Island (Střelecký ostrov), the destination of trippers in Prague already from the 16th century. In 1890 the first celebrations of the workers' holiday – 1 May – took place here with the participation of 13,000 people. And while on the left bank of the Vltava, let us walk along the Janáček Embankment (Janáčkovo nábřeží) affording a view of the river and the spires of the Old and the New Town. Running between the embankment and the Children's Island is a navigation canal with a lock chamber along which cargo boats and steamboats sail. Prague is not particularly lucky as regards statues in the exterior of the city. Here, however, on the tip of the island below Legion Bridge, there is a bronze statue Vltava by J. Pekárek (1916) which testifies to the harmony with its environment in which a beautiful Late Art Nouveau work can rind itself in the architectural layout of a unique locality (F. Sander, 1928).

From Újezd, from the part which still forms a part of the Little Quarter, a funicular railway has run to the top of Petřín since 1891. By using it we save a walk up the steep hill and get out at the halt and the Nebozízek observation restaurant, or we can go the summit and get out below the observation tower and set out along the observation paths running to Smíchov. It will lie below us and we can easily recognize its landmark in the form of St. Wenceslas's Church.

To the north, on the bank of the River Vltava, we cannot fail to notice the 30 metres high water tower (1562). Until 1886 water from the Vltava supplied 57 fountains in the Little Quarter. Let us imagine that in 1620 Albrecht of Valdštejn visited the water tower in order to check the new pumping machine which he had had installed here. When gazing at the flood or rooftops of apartment houses and and blocks of houses we can now also only imagine that Smíchov was once just a beautiful suburb beyond the walls of Prague. The gardens and vineyards of the long-distant past stretched as far as the banks of the River Vltava. In 1320 John of Luxembourg founded a Carthusian monastery here, but all that has remained is the name of the street – Kartouzská (Carthusian). In 1725 K. I. Dienzenhofer, one of the most prominent architects of the Baroque period, built a summer palace with a garden here. In its oval interior we can take part in a „Bacchanal" when viewing the frescos by V. V. Reiner (1729). F. L. Buquoy, a descendant of the old French aristocracy and the victorius imperial general in the Battle of the White Mountain, purchased the summer palace along with the garden in 1758, planting exotic vegetation and founding a greenhouse for fig trees and others. In the late 18th century there was a tavern here and then chicory was brewed here. In 1875 one of the family of its new owners, Josef Portheim, received Prague's important cultural personalities here.

The creator of modern physics and the theory of relativity Albert Einstein worked at the German University in Prague from 1911 to 1912. He lived in Smíchov in house No. 7 in Viničná Street, on which there is a memorial tablet. Standing in the centre of the small park is the stone Bears' Fountain (J. Kohl, 1689), which once decorated the nearby Slavata Garden belonging to the descendants of the governor Vilém Slavata, thrown from a window of the Czech Court Office at Prague Castle by the rebelling Czech Estates in 1618. Rainer Maria Rilke, the famous German poet who was a native of Prague and devoted his first poems to this city and the Little Quarter Cemetery, lived on the slope opposite Bertramka in Švédská Street. This runs into the street called Na Hřebenkách. If we walked from here for fifteen minutes we would come to the former kennels where Jaroslav Hašek, the genius of Czech and in fact also world humour, tried to maintain his problematic existence.

Our cultural and historical memory thus reaches as far as Prague's suburbs, but nowadays Smíchov belongs rather to the centre of the city.

Two new shopping centres were opened here recently: Anděl (Angel) and Nový Smíchov (New Smíchov).

419 The Palace of Justice in the square náměstí Kinských, originally a Neo-Renaissance barrack (1902) decorated with a cupola and statues.

420 The truncated pyramid of the **building of the Commercial Bank,** an example of modern architecture in Smíchov.

421 The only tank of Soviet production in the world to be painted pink. Now it can be seen only in a rare documentary photograph.

422 The traditional **Smíchov market** now houses a modern supermarket. The Art Nouveau exterior of the building (1908) has been faithfully restored, the responsible architect being A. Čenský.

423 The towers of the former **convent of Benedictine nuns** with St. Gabriel's Church (1891).

424 When the underground station Anděl had been constructed, the synagogue of 1863 was reconstructed.

425 The archdecanal **Church of St. Wenceslas** (1885) is a work of the prominent architect of Czech historism A. Barvitius. Its interior in the form of an Old Christian basilica is richly decorated with works by contemporary artists. Inviting you for a visit in the foreground is the Baroque **summer palace called Portheimka,** built in 1725 by K. I. Dienzenhofer.

426 The new **Strahov tunnel** was built here, which helps to solve transport problems of Prague. The photo shows the beginning of its construction.

427 The front wall of the former **Ringhoffer wagon works** was incorporated into the building of modern shopping centre.

421

428 Let no one take fright from the construction activity and bustle of traffic along the way from Anděl to Mozartova Street. Here, in the villa Bertramka as the guest of the Dušeks, W. A. Mozart completed his opera Don Giovanni (1787). The atmosphere of a cultural and natural oasis still surrounds this former agricultural homestead, which was converted into a Classical suburban villa in the mid–18th century.

429 The park and terraces are separated from the surrounding world by the gate to **Bertramka,** where concerts of classiccal music take place.

430 The garden of Bertramka is decorated with a sala terrena with paintings of 1700 and 1780 and a **bust of W. A. Mozart** (T. Seidan, 1876) which recalls the fact that the composer was a guest here again in 1791. It also reminds the visitor that in the building there is a memorial hall which is devoted to Mozart and contains original documents.

431 Bertramka was named after the owner of the one-time homestead F. Bertramský. In addition to a bedchamber, the composer F. X. Dušek and his wife also prepared a study with a piano for W. A. Mozart. In actual fact it is a beautiful music salon which, after the reconstruction of the building (1956), was provided with period furniture from the collections of the Music Museum. F. Dušek (1731–1799) was a composer and pedagogue.

431

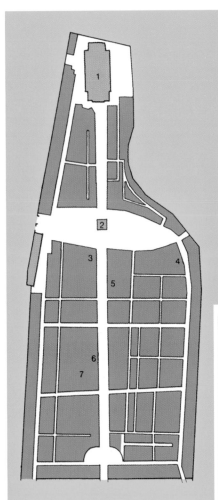

The Little Quarter Cemetery

Plan of its original arrangement

1 The cemetery church consecrated to The Holiest Trinity
2 Leopold Leonhard Count Thun-Honenstein
3 Statue of an angel
4 The Dušek family, František Xaver, composer, Josefina, opera singer
5 Adolf Kosárek, painter
6 Gravestone of a child
7 Tomášek Václav, composer

In the course of the years the graves of some prominent personalities were re-located.
The whole environment of the original cemetery has had to make way to a considerable extent for modern communication construction and the cemetery is now a small island of greenery and peace in the middle industrial Smíchov quarter.

432 Situated a short distance from Bertramka in westerly direction, between Plzeňská and Vrchlického Streets, is a quite special cemetery with graves from the Classical period (late 18th and first half of the 19th century). Although situated in Smíchov, it is called the Little Quarter Cemetery. It was founded during the plague epidemic in 1680 and from 1786 it was the public cemetery for the Little Quarter and Hradčany. **The Church of the Holiest Trinity** (1837) guards the graves, now forgotten even though many very famous people are buried here. Burials have not taken place here since 1884.

433 An **angel** covered with ivy, which is green throughout the whole year. This beautiful gravestone is just one of the group of unique sculptures in the former Little Quarter Cemetery.

434 The grave slab of F. Dušek and his wife: Here lie friends and hosts of W. A. Mozart in Prague, the owners of Bertramka.

435 Under spreading trees we walk along the paths round the gravestones and try to decipher the half-faded inscriptions and the names of the most famous persons lying at rest under them – the painters A. Mánes and A. Kosárek, the engraver V. Morstadt and the architect A. Palliardi – as well as of church dignitaries, monks and forgotten victims of the revolution of 1848.

436 The gravestone of Bishop Leopold Thun-Hohenstein of Passau

437 This gravestone of a child is one of the most poetic and the most moving.

433

434

Tele odpočívají
přátele a hostitelé W. A. Mozarta
v Praze
majitele Bertramky

FRANTIŠEK X. DUŠEK
skladatel
*6. 12. 37 v Chotěbořích +12. 2 1799 v Praze

JOSEFÍNA DUŠKOVÁ
roz. HAMPACHEROVÁ
dram. zpěvačka
*6. 3. 1754 v Praze
+8. 1. 1824 v Praze

435

436

437

189

XL PRAGUE'S GARDENS AND PARKS

Prague's oldest gardens belonged to monasteries. One of the them – the Franciscan Garden – has remained partly preserved in the very centre of the city, in the close vicinity of Wenceslas Square. Fruit trees were cultivated in monastery gardens and as regards bushes it was mainly yellow wormwood, myrrh, juniper, lavender, daphne and dogweed that were grown. Of herbs curative some plants used for dyeing purposes were cultivated. From the latter monks produced dyes for materials and for the colouring of manuscripts. A well with a spring of pure water usually stood in the centre of a garden.

Apart from monastery gardens there were numerous gardens owned by burghers in medieval Prague. On the site of Charvátova Street of the present, approximately in the place where Národní třída Station of the underground railway is situated, there was a large garden belonging to a goldsmith named Johl and in the place now occupied by Prague's main post office there was a garden owned by Mr. Angel of Florence, the friend and court pharmacist of Charles IV. Aromatic plants grew in Mr. Angel's garden and the royal apothecary sold them in his Old Town pharmacy.

The first Renaissance gardens originated in France, finding their way to Prague during the reign of Ferdinand I in 1533 when this ruler purchased several plots of land on the plain near Prague Castle and on the slopes of Stag Ditch in order to found the Royal Garden. In the spring of 1537 he received his first consignment of seeds and seedlings, which meant the beginning of the building-up of the Royal Garden in Prague. Correspondence preserved from that time witnesses the fact that Ferdinand I had an exceptional ability for gardening and personally supervised the founding of gardens.

Natural or artificial modelling of the terrain is typical of all Baroque gardens and Prague was really ideal for them. Thus it is not sup rising that a number of fairy-tale Baroque gardens originated in it in which flowers which had previously been popular in large chateau gardens began to be concentrated in a special part devoted not only to home flora, but also to popular bulb plants imported from Asia Minor.

Among Prague's most picturesque Baroque gardens are those spreading out on the site of former vineyards at the foot of Petřín. They include, for example, the garden of Jan Josef Count of Vrtba and the garden of Schönborn Palace. A legend about Vrtba's garden tells us that it was founded for a certain nymph from Petřín.

Petřín, the highest of Prague's seven hills, is itself a large park on the site of former vineyards where there were deep forests and where the pagan Czechs made sacrifices to the gods. Prague drew the „mountain" Petřín to itself, connecting it with Ujezd by means of a funicular railway, interweaving it with enchanting paths and planting it with decorative trees and shrubs. Petřín became Prague's most beautiful park affording the most beautiful view of the panorama of the city. Another large garden on the left bank of the Vltava was the one belonging to Michna Palace in the Little Quarter and now forming a part of the rich greenery of Kampa Island.

The Baroque gardens below Prague Castle, accessible from Valdštejnská Street, were composed in such a way that on the southern slope, reinforced with small walls and connected by means of flights of steps and ramps and enriched with light pavilions and gloriets, there originated an ingenious combination of natural, artificial and technical elements for which Prague is envied by everyone. The gardens below Prague Castle are unique in the world. Each one of them creates a unique impression due to its small size and intimate character. Originally they were kitchen gardens where vegetables were also grown.

The later half of the 18th century and the early 19th century were the golden age of Prague's gardens. It was at that time that Maria Theresa issued a decree according to which the city walls were abolished and Joseph II had the four previously separate towns of Prague joined to form a single whole. This resulted in a splendid opportunity for the founding of gardens and romantic parks. Gardens, parks, green promenades and oases of greenery originated not only on the sites of the former walls, but also in the communities surrounding Prague – in Royal Vinohrady, Karlín, Libeň and Holešovice. Of these gardens only smaller or larger parks have remained, for example, the Garden of Paradise (Rajská zahrada), Rieger's Park (Riegrovy sady) and Havlíček's Park (Havlíčkovy sady) in Vinohrady, the park in front of the Main Station and the one next to the National Museum.

The parks in Letná, founded by the military supplier of building materials to the Emperor Joseph II, Baron Jakub Wimmer, are living reminders of the period in question. Baron Wimmer bestowed his great wealth on Prague for the construction of gardens, parks and vineyards. Thanks to him not only gardens and parks in Vinohrady, but also the large Letná Parks on the left bank of the Vltava originated. The founder of Prague's parks is buried in charming little St. Clement's Church below the Letná plain, for whose beautifying he did so much.

The Royal Enclosure (Královská obora), or Stromovka as it is also called, was founded by Přemysl Otakar II already in the 13th century, but it was to Rudolph II that it gave the greatest pleasure. He had a tunnel dug below the Letná plain into this large forest area in order to secure sufficient water for its ponds. Still today it conducts water from the Vltava to the Stromovka ponds, representing a living monument to its founder and builder.

Contrary to the Royal Enclosure, the Star (Hvězda) Enclosure is not of medieval origin, having originated in the Renaissance period. In the Thirties of the 16th century Ferdinand I of the Hapsburg dynasty made use of the forest called Malejov, which had belonged to the Břevnov Monastery since time immemorial, for its founding. In 1556 the construction of a summer palace was completed and from 1541 to 1563 a wall with two gates – Břevnov Gate and Liboc Gate – was built round the enclosure.

Round the royal Belvedere summer palace are the Chotek Parks (Chotkovy sady), named after their founder, the supreme burgrave of the Czech kingdom Karel Chotek. The park area was opened to the public in 1841 and in 1891 the remarkable monument to the poet J. Zeyer, the work of J. Maudr, was placed here.

Prague's greenery also includes the greenery of the city's cemeteries. In the Middle Ages burial grounds originated in the immediate vicinty of churches. In 1786 Joseph II forbid this method of burial for health reasons and new cemeteries began to be founded outside the town. After the issuing of the Tolerance Patent new, separate Jewish cemeteries and inter-confessional burial grounds were established in Prague. Military cemeteries also originated.

The central Olšany cemetery covers an area of nearly 50 hectares some 80,000 graves and tombs and over 8,000 urns and columbria. Originally it was a plague cemetery founded in 1680 round St. Rochus' Church. Several cemeteries of honour containing the remains of soldiers who fell in the two world wars are located here.

In the neighbourhood of the Olšany Cemeteries is also the New Jewish Cemetery of 1891 with a Neo-Renaissance hall of ceremonies where there is a house of prayer and rooms for the ritual preparation of burials.

Of the cemeteries which remained after burials were forbidden in the town mention is deserved by the ancient little cemetery below the Letná plain, by St. Clement's Church. It is situated on the territory of old Bubny and to be seen in it are the gravestones of V. Práchner of the early 19th century, a Baroque statue of St. John Nepomuk and a polychromed gravestone of the heroic inhabitant of Prague V. Hora, who in 1866 burned a bridge to hold back the enemy at Žitavy and lost his life in doing so.

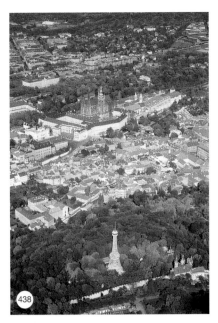

438 Aerial view of Petřín, the Little Quarter and Prague Castle.

439 The funicular railway has run up and down Petřín since 1891.

440 A Baroque vase with the emblem of the Czech crown.

441 Until 1932 this site was occupied by the Újezd barracks where **J. Neruda**, poet, writer and journalist, was born on 9. July, 1834. This great native of the Little Quarter is recalled by a memorial at the foot of Petřín.

442 The monument of the **poet K. H. Mácha,** known especially for his poem May (Máj), is the frequent destination of young people in love. The sculpture is the work of J. V. Myslbek.

443 The main reason why Charles IV had the Hunger Wall built lay in defence, but when hunger broke out in 1361 due to increasing unemployment many people found work on its construction and so it began to be called by the name we still know today.

444 The sculptor J. Mařatka began under Rodin in Paris. He was an impressionist and lyricist. And his group of **statues The Kiss** is also lyrical.

445 In 1927 the adapted little house clinging to one of the bastions of the Hunger Wall began to serve the astronomer Štefánik.

446 **St. Lawrence's Church.** In the early Middle Ages there was a place of execution by it.

447 Prague's mini-Eiffel Tower is five times smaller than its two years older sister in Paris. The construction of the Petřín observation tower was started in 1891 on the occasion of the Provincial Jubilee Exhibition.

448

448 Terraced Vrtba Garden is the work of F. M. Kaňka. Its sculptured decoration came from M. B. Braun's workshop. It consists of a large group of statues of antique gods and vases with small relief scenes.

449 From the high supporting wall of **Baroque terraced Ledebour Garden** there is a fine view of the Little Quarter and its landmarks. In the centre is St. Nicholas's Church and on the left the sharply pointed top of the steeple of St. Thomas's Church. Ledebour Garden was laid out on an older foundation in the first third of the 18th century and about 1787 it was modified, patently after plans by J. J. Palliardi.

450 Valdštejn Garden was laid out under the supervision of G. Pieroni simultaneously with the construction of Valdštejn Palace in the years 1623 to 1629. Its Early Baroque layout was evidently designed by A. Spezza, summoned to Prague by Albrecht of Valdštejn. The sculptured decoration of the main path is the work of the Netherlandish sculptor and metal founder A. de Vries, who lived at the court of the Emperor Rudolph II in Prague. At the end of the Thirty Years War the original sculptures were taken to Sweden as war booty. The most valuable garden structure from the architectural viewpoint is the sala terrena, created by A. Spezza in the style of the Italian Late Renaissance.

451 In 1918 the Castle became the seat of the President of the Republic and many of its interiors were adapted and modernized for the purpose. The architect chiefly concerned was J. Plečnik of Slovenia, who, among other things, lent the Garden on the Ramparts (Zahrada Na Valech) a new appearance. The photo shows the view from this garden of the rooftops of the Little Quarter. In the centre is St. Thomas's Church, one of the biggest and the most richly furnished churches in Prague.

452 The Olšany cemeteries were founded in 1680 far beyond the town for burials of plague victims. The Baroque church consecrated to St. Rochus is situated in their oldest part.

453 J. Brožek, a technician at the Prague Polytechnical College who in 1815 designed and constructed the first steam engine and in 1817 the first steamboat on the River Vltava, is buried in the oldest part of the Olšany cemeteries.

454 The grave of the politician J. Smrkovský.

455 This granite stone was set in place in the New Jewish Cemetery to commemorate the Jews whose last journey began in the transports to the ghetto in Lodž in the autumn of 1941.

456 The final place of rest of the writer F. Kafka in the New Jewish Cemetery enjoys state protection also for its artistic value. The gravestone has the form of a six-sided crystal with the data of the deceased on the front wall. It is the work of L. Ehrmann. On the wall opposite Kafka's grave is a bronze memorial tablet commemorating Dr. M. Brod, the rescuer of Kafka's literary work and the pioneer of Czech Jewish culture abroad!

457 The burial place of honour of victims of World War I in Olšany. Among them are also the symbolic graves of legionaries.

458 „The land on which this cemetery stands is the gift of the Czechoslovak people and it is a place of eternal rest intended to honour the memory of the sailors, soldiers and airmen who are buried here" – such are the words inscribed on the marble panel in the military cemetery in Olšany.

459 The burial place of soldiers of the Red Army who fell in the battle for Prague in May 1945. Initially they were buried throughout the whole city, mostly in the present square náměstí Jana Palacha, but later they were exhumed and interred here in Olšany.

XII. THE RIVER VLTAVA

Paris has its Seine, Rome its Tiber, London its Thames and Prague its Vltava. This river forms the axis of Bohemia, people settled by the Vltava from time immemorial and Czech towns originated on the banks of the Vltava. In the Eighties of the 9th century Prince Bořivoj founded Prague Castle on the headland overlooking the Vltava and transferred his seat here from the older Přemyslid castle site at Levý Hradec. Then Prague sprang up below the Castle.

The Vltava gradually also became the first transport route. In accordance with a privilege granted by King John of Luxembourg it served for raft navigation. The period of reign of Charles IV was the golden age of the development of water economy on the Vltava. This ruler asserted a number of measures which as a whole contributed to the further development of the country and the town. For example, he prohibited the construction of further fixed weirs between the Šumava Mountains and Prague in order to ensure smooth navigation and on the 24 already built weirs he had a lock gate of a uniform width of 12 metres installed so that boats and rafts could easily float along the Vltava.

In 1340 Charles IV had a Guild of Sworn Provincial Millers established which took decisions pertaining to all matters concerning navigation on the Rivers Vltava and Elbe. This guild was actually the supreme state water economy institution possessing extensive rights. The millers ground flour in the Vltava mills and were also entrusted with state control of the river. Ascertained offences against the imperial order were punished on the spot. From the transport aspect the Vltava was connected in the north with the Elbe and in the south with the Danube by the construction of the Švarcenberk Canal. This canal of a length of 51 kilometrest mainly served for the transport of timber and salt.

From ancient times the Vltava was an important source of water and nourishment for the people living on its banks, especially for Prague, where the agglomeration was the greatest.

In 1431 a tower appeared by the mill next to stone Charles Bridge in Prague. It was not a church tower, but a waterworks one. Its top was not occupied by a bell, but by a large water reservoir. Water was pumped there from the Vltava by machines. It then flowed down and through piping made its way to the fountains in the Big Square and the Small Square in the Old Town. Not until 1582 was a similar waterworks built in London by P. Maurice, Paris gaining its first waterworks as late as 1606. And so Prague was the first.

In 1495 another waterworks tower was built in Prague, this time by Šítek's Mill. It is still standing. Crouching at its foot is the white, square building of Manes. The Šítek Waterworks was followed by the origin of the New Town Waterworks next to St. Clement's Church in the street Na Poříčí. The Lesser Town, as the Little Quarter was then called, was served by the waterworks next to Jirásek Bridge on the Smíchov bank of the Vltava.

The quality of the Vltava water changed often. Sometimes it was wholly unsuitable for drinking and gave rise to several plague epidemics. The last big plague epidemic afflicted Prague in 1713, when more than 13,000 people, i. e., nearly one third of the total population, died.

Already from the Middle Ages the Vltava also consucted waste waters from the town. It carried away solid wastes and waste materials resulting from the craft activity of dyers, tanners and butchers, the carcasses of animals and everything which accumulated in it, particularly during floods. In 1340 Prague's municipal council issued an order pertaining to the cleaning of the town and later also a firm regulation about the cleaning of the streets. In 1490 a municipal carcass-master was appointed who with his assistants collected animal carcasses.

The Vltava is the longest Czech river. Its name is alleged to be of Celtic origin. It springs near the peak called Černá hora in the Šumava Mountains and it flows into the Elbe at Mělník. The length of its flow in Prague is 30,9 kilometres. It is the widest at the Šítek Weir (330 metres) and the narrowest at the Modřany Straits (40 metres). The greatest natural depth of the course of the river is 3 to 4 metres and the average annual flow of water is 147 cu. metres per second. Twenty-three streams flow into the Vltava on the territory of Prague.

On the Little Quarter bank the Vltava has a branch which is called The Devil's Stream (Čertovka). It begins under Legion Bridge and ends by Charles Bridge It separates the Vltava from Kampa Island. The water of The Devil's Stream was used from ancient times for the drive of water mills and remarkable wooden wheels have been preserved here to the present.

The blind branch of the Vltava in Bubeneč in the north-western part of Stromovka is called The Little River (Malá říčka). The River Berounka flows on to the territory of Prague at Zbraslav and Radotín.

The Vltava served as a water route from ancient times, but not until the mid-19th century did it begin to be used for regular passenger transport. The first Czech steamboat was built by the firm of Ruston. It was called Bohemia and it set out on its test run from the Karlín harbour on 18 May, 1841. On 26 May, 1841 the Bohemia made its illustrious, historic and often illustrated trip to Dresden. The Danish writer of fairy-tales Hans C. Andersen was also a passenger on one of the first trips from Prague to Dresden.

The route from Prague to the south was not so safe. In July 1857 the steamboat of the Prague entrepreneur Winter was wrecked on it. The situation did not change until the years 1930 to 1936, when the Czechoslovak state built a dam at Vranov nad Vltavou which swelled the river and made navigation on it possible under practically all conditions. At present the sector from Prague to the place below Slapy dam (built in the years 1950 to 1954) is navigable whatever the state of the water and so trippers can travel by boat through Prague and from Prague to the north and the south.

The Vltava navigation project began to be realized systematically at the end of 1864 by the Podskalí timber merchant F. Dittrich, who later became the mayor of Prague. He had the firm of Ruston in Karlín build a steamboat, named it Praha – Prag and on 15 August, 1865 sailed the Vltava with it. The destination of the first trip was Štěchovice. The sailing speed upstream was about 8 kilometres per hour and downstream almost twice as much.

In Prague 18 bridges span the Vltava, the longest of them being the one at Zbraslav, which connects the community with the right bank of the river. The bridge for tram transport is the northernmost. It connects Partyzanská Street and Trojská Street.

The oldest bridge is Charles Bridge, built of sandstone ashlars in the later half of the 14th century. Not until the years 1846 to 1850 was the next bridge built across the Vltava. Once again it was built of stone, being intended for the railway line from Prague to Dresden. Then the era of steel suspension bridges set in. The first of them was the chain bridge named after the Emperor Franz I. Its site is now occupied by Legion Bridge. The epoch of concrete bridges began in 1908 with Hlávka Bridge running from Těšnov to Holešovice, Troja Bridge running from Holešovice to Troja opening the era of reinforced concrete bridges. The construction of Prague's bridges after World War II was started with the building of Jan Šverma Bridge, which replaced the former cable Štefánik Bridge.

The biggest post-war bridge structure in Prague is the one between Bránik and Barrandov. It forms a part of the central circuit of the basic communication system.

460 The Vltava and its bridges. Prague's oldest bridge was built of wood and was mentioned already in 1118. About 1170 the Czech queen Judith had the first stone bridge constructed on its site, but it was destroyed by flood water. In the mid-14th century it was replaced with Charles Bridge, which is still standing in Prague (the second bridge in the photo).

In the foreground is the S. Čech Bridge, whose construction was incited by the clearance of Josefov at the turn of the 19th and 20th centuries. It is the only bridge in Prague built of flat steel arches. Its Art Nouveau sculptured decoration – bronze statues of torchbearers, six-headed hydras with the emblem of Prague and other sculptures and semi-sculptures from the studios of outstanding sculptors

here. It remembers the time when F. Dittrich, a Podskalí timber merchant and later Prague's mayor and the founder of passenger navigation on the Vltava, lived here. The houses on the embankment originated after the clearance of Podskalí and the regulation of the banks of the river in the early 20th century, at the time when some rafters exchanged their rafts for steam navigation service.

462 Water mills existed on the Vltava from time immemorial. Millers ground flour in them and from the time of Charles IV they also had the right and duty to keep watch over the river. Apart from this, they had to fulfil another task from 1431: waterworks construction and maintenance. It was then that the first waterworks began to operate, pumping Vltava water to the fountains in the Old Town and the New Town.

In 1495 Prague's second waterworks tower was built by Šítek's Mill (in the background of photo No. 522 it can be seen behind the arch of Jirásek Bridge). The next waterworks was built next to St. Clement's Church in Poříčí and given the name the New Town Waterworks. The Lesser Town, as the Little Quarter was called at that time, was provided with water by the waterworks by Petržílkovský Mill, which the local community had built in 1562. The photo shows its tower, restored in later years, on the Janáček Embankment.

of the early 20th century – is remarkable. This bridge on the left bank of the Vltava was intended to link up with the planned tunnel in the Letná slope. Situated behind Charles Bridge is the Legion Bridge (the third in the photo), connecting Národní Street with Vítězná Street in Smíchov. It is built of stone and arched with granite ashlars. It was built from 1898 to 1901 after a project by J. Janů, J. Soukup and A. Balšánek. It replaced the steel hanging Franz I Bridge of 1841. Visible wholly in the background is Palacký Bridge, built from 1876 to 1879.

461 The harbour of the Vltava flotilla by Palacký Bridge remembers the beginnings of boat trips on the Vltava and also the time when a characteristic community of rafters, woodcutters and fishermen – Podskalí – existed

463 Prague's architecture forms a charming whole with the Prague valley, which is surrounded by hills and through with the River Vltava flows. The beauty of the city originated through the harmony of the work of nature and Man. The hills round the city and the tower buildings afford an endless number of panoramatic views, but the most beautiful one of Prague Castle, Petřín and ancient Charles Bridge can be obtained from the Smetana Embankment.

464 The harbour of the Vltava flotilla between Palacký Bridge and the railway bridge. In the background is Vyšehrad with the pseudo-Gothic chapter Church of SS. Peter and Paul, rebuilt after a design by J. Mocker at the turn of the 19th and 20th centuries. Behind the arch of the railway bridge is the Vyšehrad tunnel connecting Podskalí and Podolí.

465 Prague's weirs were the oldest structures on the River Vltava. Originally they had a wooden skeleton with a stone filling and raft sluices making it possible to float timber along the river. There are five big weirs on the Vltava in Prague, some of which have retained their original appearance and form.

The weir in the photo is called Šítkovský. It originated in the Middle Ages and was named after J. Šítek, a miller.

The River Vltava is the widest – 330 metres – here.

466 The first waterworks began to originate in Prague already in the 15th century. They were built on a simple principle. On the ground-floor there was an engine room from where Vltava water was pumped into a reservoir situated on the top floor of the waterworks tower. From here the water dropped on the gravity principle and flowed through piping to the public fountains and later also Prague's houses. **The Old Town Waterworks,** built in 1489, is one the oldest waterworks in Europe. In the course of its transformation to steam drive in 1863 the administrative building of Prague's waterworks was built immediately above the level of the Vltava in the style of the Czech Renaissance, the architect concerned being A. Wiehl. Its graffiti-decorated façade is the work of F. Ženíšek and M. Aleš. The waterworks building has housed the B. Smetana Museum for a number of years now. Exhibits documenting the life and work of this composer, conductor and music teacher can be seen in it. They include the original piano of the composer of the symphonic poem The Vltava and the creator of Czech national music.

464

465

466

XIII. THEATRICAL PRAGUE

Theatre was performed in Prague already in the 12th century. It was liturgical theatre and its presenter was the George Convent at Prague Castle. The Hussite wars interrupted this dramatic activity of the church and theatre performances were not staged until the early 16th century in connection with humanistic schools. They were mainly plays performed publicly in the Carolinum, in the Greek College in the Old Town and in other buildings of Charles University. In 1558 the Jesuits commenced theatre activity in Prague, the centre of the theatre of their order being the newly built Clementinum.

The 17th century was characterized by occasional solemn performances. For example, the first ballet was staged in Prague on the occasion of the coronation of Ferdinand III. In the Seventies of the 17th century chateau theatres originated in Prague – in Valdštejn Palace and in Thun Palace and in the early 18th century Count Š: pork opened the first public theatre in his palace in the street Na Poříčí where, apart from operas, plays were also performed from time to time.

Prague's oldest municipal theatre was the one in Kotce, built by the Prague magistrate's office. The building of a permanent municipal theatre in the Old Town of Prague and its opening in 1739 was a part of pan-European theatrical development, in which Italian opera dominated, but also the result of the endeavours of forty years of Prague's lovers of this opera of operas. The basis impulse for the more permanent presentation of operas in Prague was the performance staged on 28 August, 1723 in the Riding-school of Prague Castle on the occasion of the coronation of Charles VI as Czech king.

From then on the inhabitants of Prague retained the idea of founding a permanent theatre. Prague's first municipal theatre originated on the site previously occupied by a large market hall, which in no way lagged behind the renowned cloth markets in the Netherlands. It stood where the little street called V Kotcich is now situated. The beginnings of the stage equipment were connected with the name of the then most illustrious Czech painter V. V. Reiner. The theatre allegedly had six sets designed by him. Prague became the base of Italian opera beyond the Alps. From Prague, from the theatre in the street V Kotcích, Italian artists made their way further north to Dresden and Leipzig.

In 1781 František Antonín Count Nostic-Rieneck began negotiations regarding a permit in respect of the building of a new theatre, this meaning the beginning of the end of the V Kotcích Theatre. The last performances were given here in the 1782–1783 season. From 1783 the curtain was regularly raised in the new, big „Count Nostic National Theatre" which was erected in the then ruling Classical style in the close neighbourhood of the street V Kotcích.

The Nostic Theatre originated at the cost of Count Nostic-Rieneck at the time when several of Prague's aristocrats tried to raise the cultural level of Prague in opposition to imperial Vienna. And so thanks to one of them Prague acquired a theatre building whose façade bears the dedication Patriae et Musis (To Our Country and the Muses). In 1797 the Nostic Theatre became the property of the Czech Estates and that explains why it began to be called the Estates Theatre.

In 1786 the Hut (Bouda) Theatre, also called the Patriotic (Vlastenecké) Theatre, originated in Wenceslas Square in Prague in connection with the literary and dramatic work of the brothers Thams. When it was demolished in 1789 the theatre ensemble of the Patriotic Theatre moved to the abolished At the Hiberians (U Hybernů) Monastery, where it was active until the early 19th century.

The first third of the 19th century was characterized by the gradual professionalization of actors. They gave performances in the Estates Theatre, in the previously mentioned monastery and the monastery of the Theatine order in present Nerudova Street in the Little Quarter. Their activity was connected with that of the main representatives of Czech revival drama: V. K. Klicpera, J. N. Štěpánek, and J. K. Tyl. The aim of these artists and all theatre enthusiasts was to create new Czech national theatre which would mainly serve Czech drama, Czech opera and Czech ballet.

The endeavours to achieve a Czech theatre stage culminated in 1850 with the founding of the Society for the Founding of Czech National Theatre, which organized national collections for its construction. In 1882 the Provisionary Theatre was opened with a presentation of V. Hálek's play King Vukasin. This building was later incorporated into the rear tract of the National Theatre. The professionalization of Czech theatre culminated in all spheres in the Provisionary Theatre. For example, opera presentations were connected with the activity of the conductor and Czech national composer B. Smetana.

The National Theatre, built from collections, began to be popularly called The Golden Chapel because it was not merely a theatre, but one of the Czech symbols and national shrines. Sadly, on 12 August, 1882, when its construction „was nearly completed, it" was destroyed by fire, following which newspapers were published in a black frame with the burning headline: „Mourn country, the Great National Theatre Has Burned." And collections were made for its reconstruction. Everyone contributed something, both the rich and the poor, and the theatre was rebuilt. This great collection activity is brough to mind by the gold inscription „The Nation to Itself" in the theatre proscenium. The nation built the National Theatre and had it decorated by the leading artists of that illustrious period. The architects concerned with the construction of this Neo-Renaissance building were J. Zítek and J. Schulz.

Another theatre building in Prague was the German Theatre (Neues Deutches Theater), which now serves the State Opera. It was built by Germans living in Prague on the site of the former New Town walls.

From the mid-19th century theatre was performed in wooden arenas in the summer seasons, for example, in Pštroska, Kravín and numerous other arenas in Vinohrady, in the arena in Smíchov and in permanent suburban theatres, for instance, in the Švanda Theatre in Smíchov and the Uranie Theatre in Holešovice, which began its activity on the exhibition ground in Stromovka.

In 1907, when the Municipal Theatre was built in Royal Vinohrady, Prague gained a new representative theatre in which an outstanding dramatic ensemble performed.

In the period between the two world wars many smaller theatres originated in Prague – the Liberated Theatre of J. Voskovec and J. Werich, where the composer J. Ježek worked, the O. Nový's Theatre, the theatre of the „king of comedians" V. Burian and the D 34 Theatre of E. F. Burian. All of them were situated in the centre of the city.

Theatres for children also originated. In 1920 the sculptor V. Sucharda founded the The Realm of Puppets, which still gives performances in the building of the Municipal Library. In the same year „Daddy Špejbl", the first of the puppets of the Špejbl and Hurvínek Theatre, came into being.

The war suppressed theatre activity. In the Sixties, when so-called small theatre forms originated, the Theatre on the Balustrade (Divadlo Na zábradlí), the Semafor Theatre, the Theatre Beyond the Gate (Divadlo za branou), the Rokoko Theatre and the Drama Club (Činoherní klub) were the most outstanding.

During the Eighties theatre activity spread widely also to the suburban parts of the city – the Bráník Theatre, the Klicpera Theatre in Kobylisy (now the Selesianské Theatre), the Žižkov Theatre, the Na Chmelnici Theatre and others. Apart from these, numerous new amateur dramatic societies originated.

467 The Estates Theatre (Stavovské divadlo) was built in Classical-Baroque style at the cost of the supreme burgrave of the Czech Kingdom F. A. Nostic-Rieneck. Later it became the property of the Czech Estates. The theatre is memorable due to the fact that on 29 October, 1787 the world premiere of Mozart's opera Don Giovanni took place in it. C. M. von Weber worked at the theatre as conductor of the orchestra and in 1834 J. K. Tyl's play Fidlovačka was performed during which the song Where Is My Home, now the Czech national anthem, was heard for the first time.

468 The State Opera House. This Neo-Renaissance building was erected for the New German Theatre from 1886 to 1888.

469 The Theatre on the Balustrade (Divadlo Na zábradlí) ranks among Prague's small theatres. From 1960 to 1968 Václav Havel, the former president, worked here as a stage technician and later as a dramaturgist. In 1963 his play The Garden Party had its premiere here.

470 In 1983 The New Stage was opened next to the historic building of the National Theatre. Its wall facing Národní Street is built of panels of dethermal glass. The façade neighbouring with the historic building was constructed from massive glass shaped pieces. A small triangular square originated between the old and the new building of the National Theatre which is decorated with a bronze statue of Rusalka (water nymph) by J. Malejovský. The New Stage has a circular auditorium with a stage in its centre.

471 Czech puppet theatre has a long-standing tradition. The Špejbl and Hurvínek Puppet Theatre originated in 1920 with the birth of „Daddy Špejbl". His son Hurvínek saw the light of the world through the realization of a design by J. Skupa, the principal of the theatre, in 1926.

472 The Black Theatre (Černé divadlo) reaps successes not only in Prague, but also on numerous foreign tours.

XIV. HOSPITABLE PRAGUE

Prague is well-known for its hospitality, whose tradition reaches far back into the Middle Ages. Some public houses, restaurants, taverns and taprooms remember times way back in the past. Many are renowned for the specialities on their menu and others for the drinks they serve, the typical decoration of their interiors, or the romantic legends attached to them. When visiting Prague it is really worth visiting these places for refreshments and pleasure.

Opposite the Old Town astronomical clock, in the ancient house called At the Blue Star (U Modré hvězdy), there is a small public house called U Bindrů, whose beginnings date back to the early 15th century. By walking along Melantrichova Street we come to the Coal Market (Uhelný trh) where a halt should be made in front of the house called At the Three Golden Lions (U tří zlatých lvů). A memorial tablet on it tells us that the composer W. A. Mozart stayed in it. He used to go to the nearby brewery called U Šturmů, which no longer exists, in order to play billiards. His librettist Lorenzo da Ponte stayed at the oppositely situated house called Platýz. After walking along Skořepka Street we find ourselves in front of the façade of the former brewery called U Sladkých. Situated further on is the famous Renaissance Old Prague house called U Vejvodů, restored in an excellent way in the early 20th century by a pupil of M. Aleš, the academic painter B. Klusáček. U Vejvodů is a cosy restaurant and wine tavern whose indisputable ancientness is enhanced by the stylish pseudo-historic paintings on its walls. Standing at the end of Liliová Street, at the place where it runs into Karlova Street, is the house called At the Blue Pike (U modré štiky). There used to be a tap-room here which according to a legend King Václav IV was fond of visiting in the company of Prague's executioner and the clown and magician Žito. Prague's first coffee-house was situated in the house called At the Snake (U hada) in Karlova Street.

The Little Quarter has preserved its historic public houses, tap-rooms, cafes and wine taverns better than the Old Town. It is said that the Little Quarter people were always more in favour of a quiet halt and rest than the inhabitants of the Old Town. However, here too, in the Little Quarter, all the three first international hotels in the Little Quarter, where there was also rooms for the local „regulars", have disappeared. They were The Golden Unicorn (Zlatý jednorožec) in Maltézské Square, known for the stay of L. van Beethoven at it, the hotel called In the Baths (V lázních), where the French poet F. R. Chateaubriand stayed, and the hotel called At the Three Bells (U tří zvonků).

As regards wine taverns, particularly the one called Valdštejnská, situated on the corner of Tomášská Street and Valdštejnské Square, At the Patron's (U mecenáše) wine tavern in Malostranské Square and the one bearing the name At the Painters (U malířů) in Maltezské Square try to emphasize their ancient origin by means of stylish furnishings. Each of them has a rich history interwoven with numerous legends and characteristic interior decorations.

The interesting Little Quarter restaurants definitely include the taproom of the St. Thomas Brewery and the hotel called At the Three Ostriches (U tří pštrosů), which also has a restaurant.

The St. Thomas Brewery lies in Letenská Street and the hotel called At the Three Ostriches stands where Charles Bridge runs into bank of the Vltava in the Little Quarter.

Also renowned in the Little Quarter is the tap-room called At the King of Brabant below the New Castle Steps (Nové zámecké schody). Hidden on the slope of Petřín, near the upper station of the funicular railway, there is a restaurant called Nebozízek with ancient wine cellars.

Thanks to S. Čech's novels The Excursion of Mr. Brouček to the 15th

Century and The Excursion of Mr. Brouček to the Moon it is the public house called Vikárka that enjoys the greatest renown. (According to the author Mr. Brouček set out on his travels from here.) It originally served the St. Vitus vicars, hence its name. From the 16th century wine from the chapter vineyards was tapped here and in the course of the passing years this wine tavern of the clergy became a wholly secular tap-room. Its romantic interior and its environs have always attracted numerous artists. Apart from S. Čech, the poet J. Vrchlický, the painter M. Aleš, the singer E. Destinová, the writer I. Herrmann (a wonderful narrator of Old Prague tales), the comedian of the National Theatre J. Mošna many others were fond of visiting Vikárka. To be found in picturesque Nový Svět in Hradčany is the characteristic restaurant called At the Golden Pear (U zlaté hrušky) and if the visitor walks round the Loretto into Loretánská Street he will certainly be attracted by the ancient public house called At the Black Ox (U černého vola).

It is generally known that the Emperor and king Charles IV introduced the cultivation of the vine and wine production in Bohemia. He had the vine brought from Burgundy, but he did not have to bring beer to Bohemia and Prague, because hops and barley, the main raw materials for its brewing, had even at his time been cultivated here since time immemorial. Hops had a good reputation already in the 13th century and Charles IV only promoted it when he forbade the export of hop seedlings beyond the boundaries of the Czech kingdom. He was a wise man and he knew what was necessary for the brewing of good beer. This explains why he also confirmed with his Golden Bull the ancient privilege of all respectable burghers to brew beer, to own breweries and malt-houses and to make use of the forests. When he founded the New Town of Prague Charles IV also decreed that all the brewers in the Old Town should move into new houses. However, beer production did not come to a halt in the Old Town and the Little Quarter, but it had to face the strong competition of the new breweries and brewers in the New Town. Prague gradually became a beer-brewing metropolis in whose tradition Prague's three biggest breweries – the Staropramen Brewery in Smíchov, the Braník Brewery and the First Prague Burghers' Brewery in Holešovice – now follow. Public houses and restaurants selling their branded beers are scattered throughout the whole of the city.

However, let us return to the year 1499, when the brewer V. Skřemene, or also Křemenec, founded a new brewery in an old beer-brewing house in present Křemencova Street in the New Town, now called At the Fleks (U Fleků) after its later owners. This was at the time when beer disputes arose between the aristocracy, which demanded that it be permitted to brew beer, and the burghers, who already possessed a previously granted right to brew beer. It was then that the history of the most renowned New Town brewery, At the Fleks, began to be written. In 1762 J. Flekovský purchased the brewery just at the time when the aristocracy enforced the fall of the last privileges of the beer-brewing burghers, most of whom were obliged to stop their activity in this sphere. However, the At the Fleks brewery continued to brew beer, because the local brewers succeeded in finding a way of asserting themselves and of maintaining the production of the brewery.

The literary tradition of Hašek's novel The Good Soldier Švejk gave rise to the public house called At the Chalice (U kalicha) in the interiors of a house in the street named Na bojišti. Its decoration, including the renowned painting of the Emperor Franz Joseph I thanks to which the landlord J. Palivec found himself in prison, is connected with the writer Hašek and his character Švejk.

473 This house in Husova Street first of all had a navy in its sign. In the 16th century it acquired a black lion which in the early 18th century was changed for a golden tiger. The provincial prosecutor A. L. Camillus had it set in place here, in the Middle Ages a tiger, the symbol of the new moon, was regarded as a brutal tyran and the embodiment of war. It was the European coffee-house fashion that finally inspired Prague's tradesmen to keep peace with other towns and use a tiger in their emblems. This unpleasant beast of prey first appeared on this house in Husova Street and then in Břetislavova Street on the house called At the Seven Candlesticks (U sedmi svícnů) in the Little Quarter. In the Thirties and Forties of the 19th century students, writers and drama experts went to Soch's coffee-house called **At the Golden Tiger** (U zlatého tygra) at No. 17 in Husova Street to read the newspapers and chat. The originally Romanesque building, whose last reconstruction was realized in the first half of the 19th century, now houses an Old Czech restaurant serving Pilsner Urquell beer.

474 **Beer** was a popular drink among Czech kings. The Emperor Rudolph II also drank beer. It was prescribed to him by his court physician, the natural historian and mathematician T. Hájek of Hájek. The aim of Hájek's treatment was clear: to secure the recovery of the body by means of beneficial liquid. For Rudolph II beer was one of the elixirs of life, while for Prague it is one of its longstanding attributes.

475 **Prague at night** also has its own colourful character, based on the tradition of old dance-halls and cabarets, which it now attires (or does not attire) in more modern costumes.

476 **The U Fleků Brewery** was founded in the year „of the Lord 1499" according to the inscription written in pseudo-Gothic letters. This brewery in Křemencova Street was really founded at the very end of the 15th century, but it was not until 1762 that it began to be called U Fleků (At the Fleks), when it was purchased by J. Flekovský. In the Forties of the 19th century a new tradition – the brewing of dark lager beer in the Bavarian manner – was founded here. Use ceased to be made of the former upper fermentation method and the so-called lower fermentation process was applied, lending the produced beer greater vigour and durability. With its first dark brew in 1843 the brewery entered the new industrial age.

XV. THE ENVIRONS OF PRAGUE

There are several enclaves in the environs of the historic centre of Prague which deserve the attention of visitors. One of them is the area of Břevnov Monastery, which was founded in the late 10th century. When Přemysl Otakar II defeated King Bela of Hungary in 1260 and had the remains of one of the most popular saints of the Middle Ages, St. Margaret, brought to Břevnov Monastery it began to be called At Margaret's. The monastery and its church concealed testimonies to their existence of one thousand years for a long time. Not until the middle of the present century was the pre-Romanesque crypt of the church discovered below the high altar of St. Margaret's. It was built shortly after the arrival of the Roman monks delegated by St. Adalbert, who founded the monastery. Remainders of the Gothic monastery church, the cloisters, the monastery wells and the interiors of the monastery were found.

During the Hussite wars Břevnov Monastery was attacked, burned and demolished. For a long time it remained in a state of desolation. Not until 1449 was it repaired. After the Thirty Years War a new monastery was built, but four years later it was destroyed by fire. Once again it was replaced with a new, temporary one which in the early 18th century made way for an ostentatious monastery seat built by K. I. Dienzenhofer.

On 8 November, 1620 the Battle of the White Mountain took place to the west of Břevnov, the event which decided the destiny of the Czech land for a whole three centuries. In this battle Catholic troops defeated Protestant ones and the last fight was waged by the wall of the enclosure which is now called Hvězda. Concealed in the enclosure is a characteristic summer palace which the son of the Emperor Ferdinand I, the imperial governor in Bohemia Ferdinand of Tyrol, had built in the years 1555 to 1557. The latter also designed the unusual star-shaped ground-plan after which the summer palace was named. The stucco decoration in the interior of the Hvězda summer palace, the work of unknown Italian masters, is a beautiful sample of Renaissance art. A chapel consecrated to St. Wenceslas used to stand on the White Mountain (Bílá hora). It was founded soon after the notorious battle, but in the 18th century a Catholic place of pilgrimage with a quadratic cloister, four corner chapels and a central house or prayer was built on its site.

The Royal Enclosure, also called Stromovka, is a starting point for an excursion on foot to Troja. The community of Troja was originally called Zadní (Rear) and Horní (Upper) Ovenec and it gained its new name after the chateau built from 1679 to 1685 for Count V. Vojtěch of Šternberk and his wife Klára. Count Šternberk did not choose this site below ancient vineyards amidst beautiful scenery merely by chance. For the construction of the chateau he summoned the outstanding Burgundian architect G. B. Mathey, who was schooled in Rome and who erected numeous secular and sacral buildings in Prague. G. B. Mathey built a chateau in which he adapted the Renaissance type of Roman country villa to the new ideas of the Baroque, thus bringing a new outlook on art to Prague. A remarkable sculptured supplement or this magnificent building is the exterior oval staircase decorated by the sculptors Jan and Jiří Hermann of Dresden. It portrays the victory of the Olympic gods over the Titans. Also situated here are busts of antique gods, clearly works from the workshop of the brilliant sculptor J. Brokoff.

Great attention was devoted to securing harmony between the chateau and its garden. The latter, laid out in French style, has a star-shaped system of paths with vistas in the direction of the central part of the chateau. The balustrade is decorated with large vases of fired clay with busts of Roman Emperors and heraldic Šternberk and Malzan motifs.

The Flemish artists A. and I. Godyn participated in the fresco decoration of the chateau. The grandiosity of A. Godyn's work can best be judged in the main hall, where there are scenes from the history of the Hapsburg dynasty.

The entrance to Prague's zoological garden, founded in 1931 by the traveller and zoologist Professor J. Janda, is situated in the neighbourhood of Troja Chateau. Its environment is unique in Europe, being characterized by natural rocks, lowland by the river with marshes, slopes and an upper windy area. Added to all this is old, romantic forest growth and everything is situated in an amphitheatre facing south. The rarest animals in Prague's ZOO include the Przewalski horse. An international breeding book is kept in Prague in respect of this threatened species and Prague's ZOO was the place of birth of more than one half of all Przewalski horses bred in captivity.

A trip to the south from the centre of Prague can lead to Zbraslav. The hunting court of Přemysl Otakar II, which Václav II bestowed on the Cistercians for the building of a monastery, was originally situated here. It was intended to serve as the place of burial of the Přemyslids and Václav II, Václav III, the consort of John of Luxembourg and the mother of Charles IV, Queen Eliška and the son of Charles IV, King Václav IV, really were buried here. The foundation stone of the monastery was laid in 1297. The Zbraslav Chronicle, an important source of Czech history of the turn of the 13th and 14th centuries, was written here.

The monastery Church of Our Lady and the monastery buildings, completed in 1333, were destroyed by the Hussites and after their renewal they were considerably damaged during the Thirty Years War. The church ceased to exist, its ground-plan being discovered in the course of archeological research. Zbraslav Monastery was renewed from the mid-17th to the mid-18th century. In 1785 it was abolished and converted into a sugar refinery. From 1911 to 1925 it was gradually restored for Cyril Barton of Dobenín after a plan by D. Jurkovič and A. Čenský. The outer courtyard with out-buildings, the convent, the prelature (later a chateau) and St. James' church connected with it lie in the valley on the right bank of the original bed of the River Berounka. Standing in an advanced position in southerly direction is a Baroque church with inner furnishings from the workshop of the Prague sculptor I. Platzer, supplemented with paintings by K. Škréta and P. Brandl. In the southern side chapel there is a Baroque altar with a copy of the painting Our Lady of Zbraslav, whose original of the latter half of the 14th century is in the National Gallery in Prague. The sculpture of Přemysl the Plougnman by J. Štursa and P. Janák of 1924 reminds the history of the Přemyslids family.

Situated to the west of the church is the former convent, whose main façade faces the river. The construction of the building was started before 1709 after a project by J. Santini and completed in the years 1724 to 1732 by F. M. Kaňka. Its interior houses an exposition of sculptures of the 19th and 20th centuries from the collections of the National Gallery.

„Opposite the renowned Cistercian monastery at Zbraslav, which is called Aula Regia, one mile from the town of Prague in the south, there is a high mountain surrounded by smaller hills on the other side of the Vltava," writes the historian B. Balbín, adding that a fine town of the old Bójs stood here and that it was the royal seat long before Prague. This report, which is more than three centuries old, was confirmed by widely conceived archeological research carried out from 1963 to 1973. Beyond all doubt it proved that the biggest Celtic oppidum in Bohemia was situated on Závist, dated in 2 to 1 B. C. Archeologists proved that on its acropolis there was a large area bringing the important sacred districts of Ancient Greece to mind and serving cult purposes. The Celtic Bój tribe, which ruled from this highly situated settlement, gave its name to Bohemia Boiohaemum = Bohemia, the name which has survived to the present in Romanesque and Germanic languages.

477 **The Old Governor's Summer Palace** in the Royal Enclosure (Královská obora) was founded in the early 15th century, but it was rebuilt in Neo-Gothic style in 1811.

478 **Libeň Château,** the former summer seat of Prague's mayors, is a Renaissance building of the later half of the 16th century, reconstructed in Baroque and Rococo styles.

479 Baroque **Břevnov Monastery** with St. Margaret's Church stands on the site of the oldest monastery in Bohemia, founded in the year 993 by St. Adalbert.

480 The so-called **Invalidovna in Karlín** was built from 1732 to 1737 after plans by K. I. Dienzenhofer, but only one ninth of the original project was realized.

481 **The château at Troja** is Prague's oldest Baroque summer palace. It was built in the later half of the 17th century for Count V. V. Šternberk.

482 The Renaissance royal Star (Hvězda) Summer Palace was built on a ground-plan of the shape of a six-sided star in the mid-16th century by Archduke Ferdinand of the Tyrol. It stands in an enclosure near the site where the Battle of the White Mountain took place on 8 November, 1620.

483 The former imposing **Cistercian monastery at Zbraslav** is an outstanding building representing the work of J. Santini-Aichl, the most important creator of the Czech Baroque. The monastery church was the place of burial of the Přemyslid rulers.

XVI. PRAGUE AT THE TURN OF THE CENTURY

From the early Nineties of the 19th century Prague gradually became a really big metropolis. It was particularly the clearance measures carried out in the individual quarters that secured the modernization of the city. From 1896 the demolition of the original medieval buildings was started after a project by the surveyor A. Hartig and the Na Františku and Petrská quarters, the environs of the Powder Gate in the Old Town, the area reaching from St. Gall's quarter to Moráň and the whole of Podskalí were successively cleared, a sewerage system and a new network of water mains being built at the same time.

On the occasion of the Provincial Jubilee Exhibition in 1891 Křižík's tramline system running from Letná to the exhibition ground was put into operation. During the Nineties of the 19th century the electrification of the widely branched tram network in the whole of Prague was realized.

About the year 1900 the centre of Prague witnessed unusual building activity. At the turn of the century Prague architecture was lent its most conspicuous form by J. Kotěra. His first building was Peterka's House in Wenceslas Square with characteristic Art Nouveau decoration. His later works include Laichter's House, Urbánek's House and his own family house in Hradešínská Street in Vinohrady.

The most sophisticated construction activity was concentrated in the historic core of the city, the architecturally most outstanding works originating especially in the street Příkopy, Wenceslas Square and the adjoining streets. As regards effect and social representation it was only the new buildings in the Old Town on the site of the former Jewish ghetto, in Old Town Square and in Pařížská Street that could compare with them. There ancient historic monuments – the Old-New Synagogue, St. Nicholas's Church, the Church of SS. Šimon and Jude and the Church of the Holy Spirit – formed the remaining points of old Prague around which blocks of houses were grouped.

At the turn of the 19th and 20th centuries Prague's architecture was very varied. It reached from historism to modern geometrical architecture. Prague's embankments and the former satellite communities and towns – Vinohrady, Žižkov, Vršovice, Smíchov and Holešovice – acquired a new appearance.

From the early Nineties the buildings of financial institutions began to be the most conspicuous in the old historic town. For example, in the years 1892 to 1894 the building of the Prague Savings Bank was erected in Rytířská Street and from 1897 to 1898 the Investment Bank and the Czech Industrial Bank with the Corso cafe, in which the social life of Prague was concentrated, originated.

The mid-Nineties saw the end of the epoch marked by the imitation of historic styles and the origin of a new building style – the Art Nouveau. The work of the architect B. Ohmann is a striking example of the transition from historism to this style. He began with Neo-Baroque buildings in Voršilská Street and continued with the building of the present Office for Patents and Inventions on the corner of Wenceslas Square and Jindřišská Street. The Neo-Baroque reconstruction of the Karlín Variete was his work and in 1896 he arrived at his first Art Nouveau works, which include the building of the Central Hotel in Hybernská Street. Shortly afterwards B. Ohmann's successor at the School of Applied Art in Prague, J. Kotěra, built Peterka's House in Art Nouveau style in Wenceslas Square (No. 772), whose striking decoration is the work of J. Pekárek and S. Sucharda.

Far more flamboyant, however, is the building of the Evropa Hotel in Wenceslas Square (formerly the Šroubek Hotel), designed by A. Dryák and B. Bendelmayer. The remarkable Art Nouveau interiors have been preserved in it.

The Art Nouveau also influenced older buildings which had previously been conceived in the spirit of historic styles by, for example O. Polívka. In 1902 and 1903 he designed the Art Nouveau department store called At the Novaks (U Nováků) in Vodičkova Street and the buildings housing the Praha Insurance Office and the Topič Publishing House in Národní (then Ferdinandova) Street.

The Main Station (Hlavní nádraží) of 1905 to 1909 was also constructed in Art Nouveau style, the architect concerned being J. Fanta. A pupil of J. Zítek and the assistant of J. Schulz, the architects who designed the National Theatre, J. Fanta projected the vestibule with a cupola, outwardly provided with a high tympanum, wedged between the two towers decorated with allegorical sculptures by S. Sucharda and H. Folkman. The waiting-room of the station was decorated by the popular painter of views of Prague V. Jansa. The clock-tower terminates with an imposing sculpture by Č. Vosmík. It has the form of a group of genies embracing a globe.

The most striking Art Nouveau building in Prague is, however, the Municipal House, built by the Prague community from 1905 to 1911 after a design by A. Balšánek and O. Polívka, winners of a public competition. They created a brilliant design of the whole building according to the diagonal rhombic building site.

The Municipal House is a school example of Prague Art Nouveau architecture. Leading artists of the time participated in its construction, painted, artistic and craft decoration and furnishings. In the middle of the first floor there is the Smetana Concert Hall decorated with sculptures by L. Šaloun and figural paintings by F. Ženíšek, A. Mucha, M. Švabinský and J. Preisler. Social rooms are situated round the first floor. The building houses a cafe, a restaurant, a wine tavern and an ale – house – all in the style which left such a strong mark on Prague at the turn of the 19th and 20th centuries.

At the end of the first decade of the 20th century another new art style – Cubism – penetrated into Prague. The architect J. Gočár built a house on the site of a demolished one called At the Black Mother of God (U černé matky boží), after which it was also named, and this heralded the arrival of Cubism in me city. It is a four-storeyed building with two attics, in which there was a cafe frequently visited by artists, and it is situated on the corner of Celetná Street and Ovocný trh. Another outstanding example of Cubism is the Diamant building on the corner of Spálená and Lazarská Streets. It was designed by E. Králíček.

The most prominent representative of Prague's cubist architecture was J. Chochol, who built dwelling-houses below Vyšehrad. Also ranking among cubist architecture are the cooperative dwelling-houses in Eliška Krásnohorská Street in the Old Town. They were built after a design by architect Novotný. However, they signalled the newly arriving post-war era.

Development came to a temporary halt during World War I. People no longer flocked into Prague to the former extent and the decline in the population and supply difficulties were negative results of the war. Public, social, artistic and political life was paralyzed, because the Vienna government strictly punished even the slightest manifestation of discontent.

Not until after 1918, marked by the fall of the Austro-Hungarian monarchy, the origin of the Czechoslovak Republic and the appointment of Prague as the capital of the country, did the city begin to flourish again.

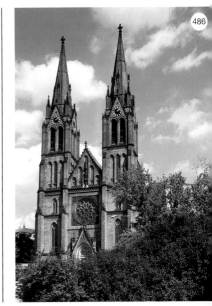

487

484 Through the building of the Municipal Theatre in Kralovské Vinohrady Prague gained a new representative building. The Art Nouveau building is the work of architect A. Čenský. Its façade terminates with two pylons with groups of statues called Opera and Drama by M. Havlíček. On the ceiling of the auditorium there is a painting Homage to the Art of Our Land, created by F. Urban. The curtain is the work of V. Županský.

485 The Vinohrady market-place was built on a slope running along Budečská Street in 1902 after a Neo-Renaissance design by A. Turek. It stands between present Vinohradská and Slezská Streets.

486 The square náměstí Míru is dominated by the Neo-Gothic **Church of St. Ludmila,** completed in 1883 after a plan by J. Mocker. With its noble appearance and due especially to its position on a slope the effect of this church surpasses that of similar works of the European Neo-Gothic. The interior decoration of the building is the work of outstanding Czech artists. The organ in the choir has three thousand pipes.

487 Detail of the glass canopy by the main entrance to Prague's Municipal House. This representative building of the society of Prague of the beginning of the century, built from 1905 to 1911 after a design by A. Balšánek and O. Polívka, combines Neo-Renaissance motifs of Czech historism with elements of the Art Nouveau and modernism. The decoration of the interior and exterior of the building is the work of recognized artists of the time (L. Šaloun K. Novák, A. Mára, J. Mařatka, F. Úprka, Č. Vosmík, K. Špillar, F. Ženíšek, A. Mucha, M. Švabinský, J. Preisler, J. V. Myslbek, E. Hallmann, M. Aleš, V. Jansa, J. Panuška and others).

Every detail of the building is brilliantly conceived as regards style, the doors, windows, balustrades, period lighting fixtures, mountings of the windows and doors, lifts with grilles, marble and wooden wall panelling, the lettering of the inscriptions, mirrors and the window glass affording proof of this. The building was newly restored.

488 In 1894 a new salon was opened in **the house of the publisher F. Topič** at No. 9 Ferdinandova (now Národní) Street where one exhibition was replaced by another. The present Art Nouveau building of the Topič Publishing house originated through the reconstruction of the original house in 1910 after a project by O. Polívka. The ceramic reliefs and sculptures on the gable are the work of L. Šaloun.

489 **The Main Station** was also built in Art Nouveau style, the architect concerned being J. Fanta. It originated from 1901 to 1903. The central hall is enclosed by two towers on which there are sculptures by S. Sucharda and H. Folkmann. The symmetrically situated lower wings of the station are terminated with towers with sculptures by Č. Vosmík.

490 Neighbouring on the building of the Topič Publishing House in Národní Street is the Art Nouveau building of **the Praha Insurance Office,** built from 1905 to 1907 after a design by O. Polívka. Polívka's architectural orientation developed from historism to the Art Nouveau style making rich use of sculptured and painted decorations. The Praha Insurance Office affords proof of this.

491 In 1893 a law was passed according to which the northern part of Old Town Square found itself on the southern boundary of the Old Town – the Josefov clearance district. In 1897 demolition work was started and at the beginning of the following century new houses originated here, for example, the building of **the Prague Muni-**

cipal **Insurance Office.** The Neo-Baroque sculptures on its façade are the work of L. Šaloun (the creator of the Huss monument in Old Town Square) and F. Procházka. The mosaic is the work of F. Urban.

492 Detail of the Art Nouveau building of **the Hlahol** Choral Society, which was built in 1905 after a project by J. Fanta after the clearance of the St. Adalbert quarter. The memorial tablet on the building commemorates three important choir masters of the Hlahol Society – B. Smetana, K. Bendl and K. Knittl.

493 In the years 1902 to 1903 architect O. Polívka designed the large Art Nouveau building of **the U Nováků** department store in Vodičkova Street. It has a two-storeyed sales court bringing the halls of department stores in Paris to mind.

494 One of the most outstanding sketchers of the European Art Nouveau, Alfons Mucha, lived in the house **V Tišině** in Bubenečská Street.

495 Cubism is a trend of art based on the principle of not presenting things as they are seen, but of portraying them in basic geometrical areas and forms. This style also found application in architecture, proof of this being the Baroque statue of St. John Nepomuk set it a cubist frame. The statue stands between the Church of the Holiest Trinity and the Diamant building in Spálená Street.

496 Cubism sometimes divided the area of a façade according to a diagonal or rays in order that the sharp edges of lights and shades might create a strong effect. In 1912 a building originated on the corner of Spálená Street and Lazarská Street which was suitably named Diamant (Diamond). It was designed by E. Kralíček and built by M. Blecha.

497 On the site of the Franciscan Garden (Františkánská zahrada), situated on an area in the immediate neighbourhood of Wenceslas Square, there was once a monastery cemetery to which access was gained through a gate decorated with a Gothic tympanum illustrating the coronation of the Virgin Mary, the figure of Charles IV and his first consort Blanche of Valois, and the Tree of Life. This valuable Gothic work was heavily damaged, thus being replaced with a modern copy. In front of the portal there is a **cubist candelabrum,** the work of the architect V. Hoffmann of 1913. It is interesting to note the harmony existing between the work of the first half of the present century and the one sculptured in the latter half of the 14th century.

498 Cubism also worked with curves. The most striking building constructed in this way is the Legiobanka, after which the cubist style is sometimes called. From the beginning of the First Republic pensions institutes and public buildings were erected in the Legiobanka style. This bank originated in the years 1921 to 1923. The historic building of the banking palace in the street Na Poříčí is an exceptional work of rondo-cubism. It is on the UNESCO list of monuments. Its monumental façade has sculptured decoration by O. Guttfreund and J. Štursa, leading artists of the time. The window glass of the bank hall is the work of F. Kysela, who also designed the painted decoration.

499

499–502 The architect J. Chochol (1880–1956) studied at the Prague University of Technology and at the Vienna Academy under O. Wagner. From decorative Constructivism he passed to spatial development and the opening of the mass or a building by using forms divided in the cubist manner. In his plastic conception of architecture, impressive with its light effects, he pointed most clearly to the connection between Czech modern architecture and the home Baroque tradition, in which Prague so richly abounds. His cubist designs were mainly realized in houses below Vyšehrad. The most outstanding of them is in Neklanova Street (photo **502**).

The enclave of Chochol's cubist buildings below Vyšehrad affords vital proof of the fact that Prague architecture did not merely remain intoxicated with the new ideas concerning art which found their way to Prague at the turn of the century, but also applied the new trends to bring about dramatic changes in the city. Chochol's buildings represent one of the most compact examples of the creative understanding of cubist architecture as a system of tectonic and spatial optical architectural elements. The triple-fronted house on the Rašín Embankment (**499, 500**) and particularly a villa in Libušina Street (**501**) are characterized by radical Cubism.

500

501

503 The architect and theoretician of architecture P. Janák was a prominent personality in the sphere of modern architecture before World War I. He trained at architectural firms in Prague, studied under the Viennese architect O. Wagner and worked in the Prague studio of J. Kotěra. Of his early work special mention is deserved by the building of Hlávka Bridge in Prague. In 1912 he and T. Gočár founded the Prague Art Workshop and from 1911 he applied cubist forms. From 1923 to 1924 he designed the family villa No. 41/484 in the street Na Ořechovce in Střešovice for the sculptor B. Kafka. It has a studio in a part of the terrace. It is built of bricks and has a steep tiled roof with dormer windows and a bust of B. Kafka is situated on its façade. Standing in the garden is a statue Orpheus by B. Kafka.

504 It is said that Střešovice is a quarter of artists and those interested would find that many painters and sculptors really did live and work here. Three artists – the painter E. Filla, the painter V. Špála and the sculptor and medallist O. Španiel – lived in the street Na Ořechovce, for example. The painter V. Beneš lived at No. 24 Cukrovarnická Street, while the sculptor B. Benda lived at No. 51. The painter M. Holý had his home and studio in Střešovická Street, the painter and illustrator V. Fiala lived in the street Na Dračkách and the painter K. Holan resided in the street Ve Střešovičkách. The photo shows house No. 755 in the street Na Ořechovce where the painter, graphic artist and illustrator V. Špála, whose work was characterized by the striking prevalence of blue, lived and worked.

505 Situated in the square Macharovo náměstí in Střešovice is the Central Building of Ořechovka, a symmetrical one-storeyed building erected in the national style in 1922. It was designed by J. Vondrák.

506 From 1903 to 1907 J. Kotěra designed a family house with a studio for the sculptor S. Sucharda. This building in Slavíčkova Street in Bubeneč manifests the tradition of English family villas.

507 This large family house in Suchardova Street in Bubeneč was designed by D. Jurkovič and it represents the artistic ideal of a Scandinavian building safely covered with a steep roof. It is somewhat bizarre in the Prague environment.

508 The Ethnographical Exhibition held in 1895 in Prague inspired a number of Czech architects. The family house of the architect J. Koula was also a creative echo of the event.

XVII. PRAGUE, THE CAPITAL OF THE CZECH REPUBLIC

The year 1918 was marked by the end of World War I, the disintegration of the Austro-Hungarian monarchy and the establishment of Prague as the capital of the new, independent Czechoslovak state. However, it cannot be said that this change of the function of the city was manifested in its architecture at once. From the architectural and urban aspects Prague had prepared for the role of the capital of the country throughout the whole 19th century, during which the Czechs endeavoured to achieve autonomy and counted with the fact that Prague would be the centre of one of the countries of federalized Austria. This process was very intensive especially in the later half of the 19th century, when the Jewish Town was cleared, when the Smetana Embankment (Smetanovo nábřeží) with a number of monumental buildings such as the National Theatre, the Rudolfinum or the Academy of Applied Art originated and when new bridges and a number of representative buildings sprang up in Wenceslas Square (Václavské náměstí), Národní Street and the street called Na příkopech.

In 1920 a State Regulation Committee was created on the basis of a law of 5 February, its activity having a substantial influence on the building-up of the capital of the republic. The imposing building of the Ministry of Railways began to grow on the Petrský Embankment (Petrské nábřeží) after a project by A. Engel, conceived in the spirit of Classical monumentalism. A. Engel constructed buildings in the round square in the Dejvice quarter. In 1924 the competition for a new building for the Working-class Injury Insurance Office in the Holešovice district was won by the avant-garde design of J. Krejcar and the projects of F. M. Černý. In the same year the construction was started of the Fair Palace in Holešovice after a design by O. Tyl and J. Fuchs and two years late the Electricity Enterprises came into being near the Fair Palace. In asserting this design the members of the jury succeeded in maintaining a project which declined away from the old block-type architecture and permitted the construction of a building on an empty site with no respect for the network of already existing streets. After this triumph another modern project originated from 1928 to 1932 in the form of the General Pensions Institute in Žižkov. Its designers were J. Havlíček and K. Honzík. In the complex of everything built in Prague at the turn of the Twenties and Thirties the palace of the General Pensions Institute meant not only a sample of high avant-garde art, but also a bold intervention in the then panorama of the city which was sharply criticized by art historians influenced by antiquarianism.

Certain important modern, separately standing buildings in various places in the city also rank in this avant-garde period. They include, for example, St. Wenceslas's Church in Vršovice, the work of J. Gočár, several schools, for instance the building of the secondary school in Dejvice in Evropská Street, the school in the square Lobkovicovo náměstí and the Church of the Most Sacred Heart of the Lord built in the square náměstí Jiřího z Poděbrad in Vinohrady by J. Plečnik from 1929 to 1932. This church, inspired by Old Christian architecture, not only forms the captivating landmark of the whole spacious square, but also occupies a conspicuous place in the panorama of Prague as a whole. The architect J. Plečnik was summoned to Prague in order to participate in the realization of extensive alterations and reconstructions at Prague Castle in such a way as to ensure that it served the representative purposes of the first president of the Czechoslovak Republic, T. G. Masaryk. The Church of the Most Sacred Heart of the Lord represents his later work in Prague.

After World War I the inner part of the city was also enriched with new, important buildings. The first indication of the new style in the centre of Prague was the department store housed in No. 8 in the street 28. října. It was designed by R. Stocker in 1920. However, its real appearance was lent it by the inseparable architects J. Gočár and P. Janák.

In the years 1921 to 1923 the palace of the Bank of Czechoslovak Legions in the street Na Poříčí was built after a design by J. Gočár. Its red-and-white, robustly articulated façade with hemispherically profiled window recesses brings Old Russian architecture to mind. The sculptured decoration of this building, the work of J. Štursa, is really outstanding. This building, inscribed on the list of cultural monuments of UNESCO, is so striking that it gave rise to the „Legiobanka style" concept and at its time it was a strong and inspiring impulse in the sphere of architecture. The Adrie Palace on the corner of Narodní Street, Jungmannovo Square and Jungmannova Street, built from 1923 to 1925 after a project by P. Janák and J. Zasche, ranks with the colourfulness of its stone façade in this epoch as well even though its general conception rather brings Italian Early Renaissance architecture to mind.

The Juliš Palace in Wenceslas Square, the YWCA building in Žitná Street and the interior of the Black Rose (Černá růže). Arcades in the street Na Příkopech are a representative of Early Functionalism. In the Thirties the architect O. Starý enriched Národní Street with the attractive Building of the Art Industry. The Thirties also saw the origin of a really modern department store in Prague. It was given the old local name of White Swan (Bílá labuť) and it was erected in the street Na Poříčí after plans by J. Hrubý and J. Kittrich.

During the period of the First Republic five new complexes of ministries sprang up from Palacký Bridge to Hlávka Bridge on the right bank of the Vltava. Due to its archaic character the ministry building in the part called Na Františku deviates from this series. It was built from 1932 to 1933 after a project by J. Fanta, based on the Art Nouveau style.

In connection with the construction of the Barrandov Film Studios the architect M. Urban designed the new Barrandov residential quarter featuring wholy individually conceived, exclusive family houses. All of them were of an outstanding architectural standard. The building of villa quarters with family houses was made possible by the laws governing construction activity adopted by the First Republic. Apart from luxurious Barrandov, the Ořechovka, Hanspaulka and Spořilov garden towns also originated. The new Prague town of Dejvice was built after a design by A. Engel and the so-called Masaryk's Houses, a township for senior citizens (now the Thomayer Hospital), originated.

The most striking building activity in Prague in the period between the two world wars was the construction of the Baba residential colony in Dejvice. From the urban aspect it was founded on the system of family houses situated round the streets following the contour lines of the old hill above the Vltava. The most outstanding architects of the time oriented their forces and abilities to the Baba residential colony, their ranks including J. Gočár, P. Janák, O. Starý and L. Machoň.

In the years 1908 to 1912 the era of concrete bridges began with the construction of Hlávka Bridge, the next to be built being Mánes Bridge, which replaced the footbridge running from the Rudolfinum to Klárov. In the post-war years, from 1924 to 1928, the construction of concrete bridges continued with the building of Libeň Bridge, linking Libeň with Holešovice, and Troja Bridge running from Holešovice to Troja (1927–1928). Troja Bridge opened the era of reinforced concrete bridges. The last bridge to be built in the pre-war republic was Jirásek Bridge (1929–1933) after a project by F. Mencl. It spans the river between Smíchov and the New Town and was designed by V. Hofman.

510

512

511

513

509 **The Church of the Most Sacred Heart of the Lord** in Vinohrady differs conspicuously from everything that originated in the sphere of architecture in Prague between the two World Wars. This monumental house of prayer, which is built of glazed bricks interspersed with ligh granite, was designed by J. Plečnik of Slovenia.
510 **The House of the Czech Union of Fire Brigades** standing on the corner of Blanická and Římská Streets was built in 1935 after an older project by architect F. Kavalír of 1926 to 1928.
511 **The House of Agricultural Edu-**

cation was designed by J. Gočár from 1924 to 1926. Inside it there is a memorial tablet commemorating the cousins Veverka, inventors of the swing-plough.
512 **The high radio-communication tower** for television, radio and telephone transmission, built after a project by V. Aulický, was completed in 1991.
513 Below the radio-communication tower is **the remainder of the old Olšany Jewish cemetery,** founded in 1680 during the plague period.

514 F. Bílek was a sculptor, sketcher, wood-carver, graphic artists and architect. His naturalistic vision was his means for expressing his mystic vision of reality. From 1895 he sometimes sojourned at Chýnov, his place of birth, near Tábor, where he built a villa with a studio. He designed and built this house in Prague which stands on the corner of Marianské hradby and Mickiewiczova Street in Hradčany.

515 The large building of the Philosophical Faculty of Charles University was designed in 1929 by J. Sakař. It is a quite original combination of the Art Nouveau and historism based on the Italian Renaissance.

516 The Rudolfinum is the work of two professors of Prague's Poly-technical University – J. Zítek and I. Schulz. This large Neo-Renaissance building was completed in 1884, being named in honour of the then Austrian crown prince Rudolph, but the public in general considers it to commemorate the art-loving Emperor Rudolph II, who resided at Prague Castle at the turn of 16th and 17th centuries. The palace was intended for concert and exhibition purposes, but during the first Czechoslovak Republic it served as the parliament. The main southern façade of the building facing the square náměstí Jana Palacha is of an arched conception. On the roof attic there are statues of composers and on the sides of the flight or steps from the square there are sculptures of seated musical Muses. In the roofed subway in the street ulice 17. listopadu there are two lions. The entrance from the embankment the western side is decorated with Sphinxes. The concert hall in the Rudolfinum has excellent acoustics. Eighteen high Corinthian columns standing on the edge of its gallery bear the ceiling, which runs towards the centre. In the centre of the rear part of the building there is a hall, illuminated from above, in which exhibitions of the Beautiful Art Union were held at the turn of the 19th and 20th centuries. Lining the streets and the embankment were exhibition halls and the clubroom of the Society of Patriotic Friends of Art.

517 In 1901 the building of **the Museum of Decorative Arts** was completed on an area taken from the Old Jewish Cemetery. It was designed in Neo-Renaissance style by J. Schulz. Its façade bears reliefs of emblems of crafts by B. Schnirch and A. Popp and on the entrance staircase there are wall paintings of allegories of crafts by F. Herčík and K. V. Mašek.

518 **Müller's villa** in the street called
Nad hradním vodovodem in Střešo-
vice is the work of the Austrian architect A. Loos. This propagator of a non-
decorative shape signalled the arrival
of Functionalism already before World
War I. The originator of the spatial
conception of an individual house designed this one in Střešovice in 1930.
Its exterior is austere, but its interior is
exclusive. The charm of the house lies
mainly in the characteristic arange-
ment of its interiors.
519 **Hübschmann's family villa.** Architect B. Hübschmann was a pupil of
the Technical University in Prague and
F. Ohmann and from 1901 to 1904 he
studied under O. Wagner at the Academy in Vienna. He fulfilled numerous
architectural and urban tasks. His own
villa dates in 1927.
520 In the Twenties between the two
world wars individual ideas on dwelling in Prague followed two trends: one
was represented by the more modest
construction of family houses, while
the other was originated to the building of comfortable villas standing in
their own garden, laid out at great
cost. **The villa of architect E. Linhart**
in the Hanspaulka quarter represents
the latter trend. It was built in functionalistic style from 1926 to 1928.

521 In 1934 **the building of the General Pensions Institute** originated on the site of a former glassworks in the northern corner of Žižkov after plans by J. Havlíček and K. Honzík, who were hardly thirty years of age at the time.

522 **The building of the Supreme Court of the Czech Republic** in Pankrác was built from 1926 to 1930.

523 **Hlávka's Bridge** (Hlávkův most) is decorated on the Holešovice side by pseudo-cubist pylons with groups of statues Work and Humanity, the work of T. Štursa.

524 On the corners of the New Town Hall in Mariánské Square there are sculptures of Rabbi Low and the Iron Knight by L. Šaloun. The photo shows the legend-woven Jewish rabbi of Prague, Jehuda ben Becalel – alias Rabbi Low.

525 **The monument of the historian F. Palacký.** The Art Noveau group of statues of bronze and sandstone is the work of three artists: the sculptors S. Sucharda and J. Mařatka and architect A. Dryák. It originated in 1912.

526 **The observation restaurant at Barrandov** forms a part of the whole designed in 1927 by M. Urban.

527 St. Wenceslas's Church in Vršovice was built after plans by J. Gočár.

528 **The building of the Electric Enterprises of Prague,** built from the year 1926 to 1927 on the northern bridgehead of Hlávka's Bridge, is the work of the architects A. Beneš and J. Kříž.

XVIII. THE YOUNGEST PRAGUE

After World War II Prague's architecture was influenced by the foreign principle known as „socialist realism", which originated in Moscow in the early Thirties. The International Grand Hotel in Dejvice, built from 1952 to 1956 after a project by F. Jeřábek and a team of workers of the Military Design Institute in Prague, is a sample of this conception of „socialist contents and national form". The ostentatious decoration of the hotel, conceived according to then contemporary principles, is the work of a number of leading artists headed by M. Švabinský, C. Bouda, A. Fišárek and I. Novák. The Jalta Hotel in Wenceslas Square is the only striking building of „socialist realism" in the centre of the city. It was built in 1954 after a design by A. Terzer.

In the early Sixties building activity was centred on the construction of „towns" with tens of thousands of inhabitants round the centre – Červený vrch, Malešice, the Novodvorská, Pankrác and Krč housing estates and later satellite towns with hundreds of thousands of inhabitants, the North, South and South-West Towns. Transport problems began to be solved at same time. After the construction of Šverma Bridge a tunnel originated under the Letná slope, the Braník railway bridge was built and a basic plan of a communication system, which was realized simultaneously with the construction of Prague's underground railway, was drafted. In this connection a bridge was built across Nusle Valley, planned already during the First Republic, and another below Barrandov. A bridge below Strahov will serve the same purpose in the future.

The post-war years were also marked by the construction of hospitals and medical facilities. Remarkable is, for example, the building of the urological clinic of Charles University in the street Ke Karlovu in Prague 2, designed by V. Růžička. The biggest post-war hospital is represented by the buildings of the Faculty Hospital in Motol, built after a design by R. Podzemný and A. Tenzer. The outstanding exterior feature of Motol Hospital are the balconies running round the floors of the in-patient departments. They also serve as sun-breakers.

The years 1966 to 1972 were marked by the heightening of the former stock exchange next to the National Museum with a new building intended to meet the purposes of the Federal Assembly of the Republic. However, the superstructure and reconstruction of the former parliament are a sample of a lack of understanding of the tasks of new architecture originating in a historic environment. Another sample of bad judgement is the construction of an arterial road running round this building and separating the National Museum from Wenceslas Square.

In the years 1971 to 1975 Prague's largest department store, The Anchor (Kotva), was built between the square náměstí Republiky and Rybná Street after a project by Věra and Vladimír Machonin.

The construction of an underground railway in Prague was planned already in the Twenties, but it was not until 1 May, 1974 that the first train set out on line C from Pankrác to Karlín. Prague's underground railway is characterized by the fact that the vestibules often form a part of subways securing the underground connection of several places in the city and also that a number of exits from the underground railway are incorporated in arcades. Particular attention is deserved by Vyšehrad Station at the southern end of the bridge across Nusle Valley. Its architecture is remarkable and it affords attractive views of Prague from the south of the Vltava Valley and of Royal Vinohrady. Standing near the Vyšehrad underground railway station is the Palace of Culture, an example of the megalomania of the communist regime. In that period it mainly served party congresses and conferences. The building was converted into a congress centre which in 2000 was the scene of a session of the International Currency Fund and Group of World Banks.

Můstek Station of the underground railway is interesting due to the fact that one arch and half another of the former bridge running across the local ditch to St. Gall's Gate (Svatohavelská brána), which was a part of the Old Town fortification system in the Middle Ages, are preserved in a restored state in its vestibule.

The fall of the communist totalitarian regime in 1989 and the following privatization process have had a strong influence on the architectural appearance of Prague. It is particularly financial institutes and hotels which are sensitively renewing old historic Buildings and building new ones. For example, the Trade bank (Obchodní banka) is having Gočár's palace of the former Legion Bank restored in the street Na Poříčí. This building is contained in UNESCO's list of historic monuments. The Commercial Bank (Komerční banka) is reconstructing a historic building in Dlouhá Street and the Genereli Insurance Office is building an eight-storeyed administrative building with a four-storeyed underground car park of 700 cars and an observation terrace on the roof on the corner of Anglická and Bělehradská Streets.

The Don Giovanni is unquestionably the most beautiful stone in the necklace of hotels which originated in Prague after 1989 and which also includes the Renaissance Hotel opposite Masaryk Station. This outstanding building of the 20th century serves as the administrative seat of the Nationale Nederlanden Insurance Company.

Known as The Dancing House, it was built at the end of 1992 after a design by Vlado Mulunič and Frank O. Gehry. It is called The Dancing House because its two towers bring the dancers Ginger Rogers and Fred Astaire to mind.

529 **The Dancing House** was the subject of numerous disputes between experts and laymen alike. Finally, however, Prague accepted the avant-garde design of the building, which gained the high award of the American magazine Time in the World Design category in 1966.

530 Baba was settled already in the Stone Age. This ruin was adapted at the time when the romantics turned to the Middle Ages and pretended that pisturesque replicas were original structures. The photo shows the ruin of a grape press, adapted to represent the ruins or a small Gothic castle. In the background is the Bohnice housing estate.

531 The Congress Centre in the Pankrác quarter of Prague was built as a Palace of Culture during the communist regime. However, it affords beautiful and unusual views of Prague from the south and from the architectural aspect it is remarkably connected with Vyšehrad Station of the underground railway.

532 A plan concerning the spreading of Prague in southerly direction originated already at the turn of the present century. However, the war years shifted this idea to the time when Prague became the capital of the new Republic. S. Bechyně and architect Kozák then drafted a project of a housing estate in Pankrác. Nusle Valley was to be spanned by a bridge substantially shortening the journey from the centre of Prague to Pankrác. Nusle Bridge (seen in the photo) originated on the basis of a group of successful designs by various engineers and architects as late as 1965. S. Bechyně, who throughout his whole life asserted the idea that reinforced concrete was the most remarkable building material invented by mankind to date, remained concealed in the team of engineers and architects. On the left in the photo is the tower building of the Corinthia Towers Hotel situated on the Pankrác bridgehead.

533 The Holiday Inn Hotel, formerly the International Hotel, in Dejvice, built in the Fifties in the spirit of „socialist realism".

534 Cubism? No. The balconies of post-war blocks of flats at **Červený vrch.**

535 The Praha Hotel was built in the Seventies for the communist party bosses.

536 At the end of World War II Emmaus was damaged during an air raid. After the war architect F. M. Černý added this concrete structure resembling the sails of a ship to the monastery church. It is a striking landmark in the locality.

537 Several tower buildings, erected in the first half of the Seventies, stand in a panoramatically exposed position in the middle of the Pankrác plain. Among them is the Panorama Hotel with an enchanting view of Prague.

538 Smíchov. The core of the new Smíchov downtown is represented with an administrative, shopping and entertainment centre built up on the place of old buildings, particularly at the place of former engineering factor Tatra Ringhofer Works. The dominant of the entire territory is the building at New Angel (Nový Ánděl) designed by French architect Jean Nouvel.

539 The Renaissance Hotel near Masaryk Station is intended for a wide business clientela and congress guests.

540 This glazed building on the corner of Anglická and Bělehradská Streets in Vinohrady belongs to the **Genereli Insurance Office.** In the underground part there is a multi-storeyed garage. From the roof terrace there is a captivating view of Prague, similar to the one which the people of Prague saw from the vineyards and promenades in the environs of the New Town walls.

541 The cement containers at **the concrete works at Kačerov** were lent a human face by the painter and designer J. Rada

542 Prague is called „the city of a hundred spires", but their actual number is far greater. This is one of the views of the spires of Prague behind the Old Town in the direction towards Petřín. The two Baroque spires on the left in the photo belong to the Church of the Holy Saviour in the Clementinum. The dominant feature on the right is the tower of the former Clementinum observatory, which until 1918 had the task of determining noon. Every day a man stood on the stone gallery and waved a flag when the hands of the observatory clock met on the twelve mark. Thereupon a cannon boomed in the street Mariánské hradby in the Letná quarter announcing that it was dinner time. Between the steeples of the Church of the Holy Saviour and the observatory tower we can see the Old Town Bridge Tower, a work of the High Gothic by P. Parléř: In the background, on Petřín, is Prague's „Eiffel Tower" – an observation tower – and the steeples of St. Lawrence's Church.

543 View of the Old Town spires from the west. In the centre are the twin steeples of Týn Church and in front of them the green cupola of the Crusaders' Church of St. Francis with its neighbour in the form of the Old Town Bridge Tower. On the right in the photo is the tower of the Old Town Hall. Seen on the left of Týn Church are the steeples of the Baroque Church of St. James, which is adjoined by a building with an intimate Gothic court of paradise. In the chapel below the uncompleted steeple of the church there is a memorial tablet recalling the guild of Old Town butchers, who on two occasions saved the church and the monastery from falling into a state of disrepair. The first time was during the Hussite wars and the second during the anti-Catholic demonstrations in 1611.

544 View of Prague from the Petřín observation tower. In the foreground is Charles Bridge with the Old Town Bridge Tower. Close to this tower are the Crusaders' Church of St. Francis Seraphinicus, the high steeples of the Church of the Holy Saviour and also the Clementinum church with the Clementinum observatory tower. Visi-

544

ble in the lower right-hand corner is the Old Town Water Tower, a Renaissance building of the later half of the 16th century. In the centre of the photo is Old Town Square, dominated by the steeples of Týn Church, the tower of the Old Town Hall and the three steeples of the Baroque Church of St. Nicholas, which originated after a project by K. I. Dienzenhofer in the Thirties or the 18th century.

The view or Prague's spires is closed in the right-hand upper corner by the Powder Tower, founded in 1475 by King Vladislav Jagiello. Due to the fact that gunpowder was stored in it in the early 18th century it began to be called the Powder Tower.

On the left of Týn Church we can see the steeples of St. James's Church, renowned for the organ concerts which take place in it.

543

Illustrated guide
PRAGUE

Second complemente edition

Photographs:	Barbara Hucková, Miroslav Hucek
Text:	Václav Cibula, Petr Chotěbor, Alexandr Kliment, Jiří Poláček, Eduard Škoda
Plans:	Petr Chotěbor
Translation:	Joy Turner-Kadečková
Language editing of the second publication:	Barbora Hlaváčová
Graphic designior the photographic part:	Miroslav Hucek
Typography:	Jiří Poláček
Publisher:	Prague Publishing House of Jiří Poláček, 2004
Pre-press:	Printing House MV Prague
Printed and Binding by:	Printing House Havlíčkův Brod